蔡潔儀

私房菜

Kitty Choi's
Private Kitchen Cuisine

蔡潔儀編著
萬里機構・飲食天地出版社出版

前言 Preface

　　"私房菜"是十多二十年前本港一些烹飪界前輩所開創的一個飲食新潮流。其賣點當然是以名廚親自下廚的拿手菜式，食客大部份是慕名而來的。"私房菜"這個名堂，彷彿已成為專業和品質的保證。

　　時至今天，私房菜的定義，隨着樓上食館如雨後春筍的誕生而有所改變。很多美其名説是私房菜，其實只是開設在私人地方的樓上食肆。

　　從小便熱愛烹飪的我，最期望實現的理想，是能為一些真正識飲識食、會説真心話的朋友親自下廚，讓他們也分享我烹飪的樂趣。

　　自從加入烹飪行列，一直以培訓烹飪人才為己任。開設導師培訓班，成功地訓練了一些可以交棒的接班人。遺憾的是過去的校舍地方有限，在教導學生時，總覺得欠缺了很多東西。正因如此，當我再重新創辦烹飪學校時，便考慮到預留空間，騰出一些地方以作私房菜訓練班之用。一者可以實現我的理想，二者可以給我的學生多一個實習的機會。我的私房菜，便是由此創立起來。

　　在我的角度來説，"私房菜"就是把我自己所學所聞的烹飪技術，融匯自我對烹飪的熱情加以創作，親自炮製出包含個人風格以供同好欣賞的佳餚美饌，這便是私房菜。

　　我的私房菜與別不同的地方，不在於食譜的改革創新，而是要求整個食製都由基本的元素做起。調味、醬料、酒與食材都要有個人風格。買回來的調料，便是大眾化口味，做不到我的要求。要達到如此水平，惟有自己親手做。

　　飲食文化有創新的需要，否則停滯不前，便不會有進步。但懷舊的菜式，亦有其歷久不衰的保留價值，為着保留傳統，我把自製素材，融入懷舊名饌之內，好讓有緣人產生共鳴，亦讓年輕人瞭解過去。

蔡潔儀

2008年・春

"Private Kitchen Cuisine"(speakeasies) was introduced by some culinary experts about two decades ago. They make use of their specialties as a feature selling point to attract customers. Over the years, this term has become synonymous with professional and quality assurance of exquisite delicacies.

Nowadays, with small dining places in apartments spread like wild fire, its use has been abused. Many of such eateries, which claim themselves to be "private kitchen", are in reality just offering ordinary cuisines in a private area.

Having discovered my passion for cooking at a very young age, I have always dreamt of sharing my pleasure of cooking with my truthful friends who appreciate good food. Ever since the beginning of my cookery career, I have been dedicated to training culinary talents by hosting cookery classes for trainers and have successfully trained up many good cooks in the course. However, due to limited space in my old cookery centre, it was not fully equipped to demonstrate a wide variety of foods. In the light of this, I specially reserved some areas for teaching private kitchen cuisine when I opened a new school years ago. Through this kitchen, I can experiment with new methods of cooking while providing a better learning and practicing environment for my students.

I think that "private kitchen cuisine" should integrate one's cooking passion and innovative ideas with various cooking techniques in creating some signature dishes. The uniqueness of my private kitchen dishes does not come from the innovation of recipes, but the discriminating demand on basic ingredients. We have to infuse our personal styles into the elements, from the main ones down to complements like seasoning, sauces and wine. If the readily made ones cannot live up to my expectations, I will prepare them by myself.

I agree that eating cultures are changing and we have to be creative in order to stay abreast of the trend. However, some old dishes are of high regards and have to be conserved. To uphold our culinary heritage, I blend my homemade sauces into some renowned dishes so that they may bring back some sweet memories for the older generations while letting the young ones learn more about the past.

Kitty Choi
Spring 2008

目錄 Contents

調味醬及酒
SEASONING AND WINE

自製調味品、醬料及釀酒

調味、醬料、料酒等，是烹調時不可缺少的基本元素，主料縱然是上佳素材，如果沒有它的輔助，也難發揮得盡善盡美。

昔日的小家庭，生活比較簡單，常用的醬料和醃菜等，很多人都喜歡自己親手做。一般家庭大多設備簡陋，沒有雪櫃儲存，做好的醬料都放在紗櫃內，可能當時的空氣沒那麼混濁，而且四季分明，只要在合適的氣候時才製作，物料放在紗櫃內也不易變壞。雖然現今市售的品牌及種類多如天上星宿，但自家製作，不含防腐劑，食得健康及安心，濃淡調配，任隨君意，把入廚也變成樂事。因此，醬料、原材料等的製作技能，對醉心廚藝人士而言，是有一定的學習價值。

在這裏，我會介紹製作兩款醬料（欖豉醬和自製南乳）和釀製四種酒（甜酒釀、客家糯米酒、檸檬酒、菩提酒）。為免用得太久而變壞，做好的醬料要貼上製作日期，也不要大量製作，應用完再做，便不會浪費。

甜酒釀除了可以做甜品和日常小菜外，餘下的酒醋，還可以用來搓包子及做點心。不只是上海人的珍品，很多廣東人也十分愛用。

客家糯米酒的製作，與甜酒釀差不多，味美而實用，並兼備補身功效，可用作婦女懷孕補身及分娩後煮雞酒之用。

　　釀製檸檬酒的靈感來自我的外太婆，老人家愛用玉冰燒，加入去了核的切片檸檬浸酒。當年買酒不用上街，會有酒販擔着盛酒的擔子上門兜售。小時候不懂事，以為是檸檬糖水，幾個小孩偷偷把糖水拿來喝，弄得面紅耳赤，才知出事，還要接受處分，吃個"籐條燜豬肉"呢！時至今天，我仍不是個愛酒之人，但我喜歡用美酒製作食物，"美酒佳餚"這個詞彙，看來不只在歡宴時合用，只要懂得活用美酒，平凡的物料也可變成佳餚。

　　第一次看到人家釀製菩提酒的時候，年紀長大了一點，不再胡亂拿來喝。那時舊居清拆，舉家遷往九龍，鄰居有一位黃太太，她的丈夫是船員，一去最少也得一年半載才回家。每當黃先生休假回家時，黃太都會親自釀製丈夫至愛的菩提酒以示歡迎。我亦因此而學會了，得益不少。

　　欖豉醬是一款甚受歡迎的醬料，因為可以煮苦瓜、蒸魚、燜雞等等，用途廣泛，而且食味一流，自製一點作日常使用，方便衛生兼可變家中廚神，很有自豪感。

　　南乳的製作比較繁複，因為要等到它發酵至起大霉菌，時間是要配合得很好，在黃梅時節才做，較為適合（此書拍攝時間未能配合，天氣較乾燥，所以霉菌出得很少，做得不大理想）。南乳是常用的物料，做菜製餅都合用，如香脆可口的雞仔餅、新年煮的齋菜、南乳花生燜豬尾、南乳豬肉燜蓮藕等，很多菜式都用得着，所以一般家庭，如懂得做的，都愛做一點放在家中。

Homemade seasoning, sauces and wine

Seasoning, sauces and wine are essential elements in cooking. Without them, even a dish of superb main ingredients will be less than perfect.

In the old days, life was simpler and people liked to make some preserved sauces and pickled vegetables at home. The air conditions were better then and four seasons were distinctive. People would make sauces in the right weather and then keep them well in cupboards for later use. Although there are now numerous ready-to-use sauces available in the market, they cannot be compared with the homemade ones, which contain no preservatives and are tailored to individual tastes. Therefore, the techniques to process sauces and basic ingredients are useful to culinary lovers.

In this section, I will tell you how to make two sauces and four wines. Including sweet glutinous rice wine, Hakka-styled glutinous rice wine, lemon wine and grape wine, as well as olive and black bean sauce and fermented red bean curds. We must label the finished products with their producing date for reference. Besides, you should not make too much at a time. Or, the sauce may go rotten over time and be wasted.

Sweet glutinous rice wine can be used to make desserts and dishes while the residual fermented glutinous rice can be used to make buns and dim-sum. It is a favourite of both Shanghai and Guangdong people.

The making of Hakka-styled glutinous rice wine is similar to that of sweet glutinous rice wine. It is not only tasty but also nutritive to expectant mothers. What's more, it can even be used to cook chicken wine for ladies after labour.

The idea of brewing lemon wine came from my great grandmother who loved to soak slices of cored lemon in Chinese white wine. When I was a kid, I stole some from her to try, thinking that it was sweet lemon juice. Unfortunately, I became drunk and was punished. From then on, I have not been into drinking and just like to use wine for cooking, turning ordinary food into fine dishes.

I learnt the making of grape wine from my neighbour, Mrs Wong, when I was older. Her husband was a sailor who came home every half a year or so. Therefore, whenever Wong was back, his wife would make his favourite grape wine specially for him.

Amongst various sauces, olive and black bean sauce is one of the most popular ones due to its versatile usage. It can be added to braised bitter melon, steamed fish and stewed chicken. It is easy to make and can help touching up the dishes.

On the other hand, the making of fermented red bean curds is more complicated. It has to be processed in humid weather to facilitate the fermentation of bean curds. It is commonly used in cooking and making biscuits, such as crunchy chicken biscuits, vegetarian dishes for Chinese New Year, stewed pig tails with peanuts, stewed pork with lotus roots, and many others.

甜酒釀

Sweet Rice Wine

時間：2小時
份量：1-2斤
Processing Time: 2 hours
Servings: 600g - 1200g

INGREDIENTS

600g glutinous rice
1 pc Chinese yeast cake
¼ cup boiling water
1 pc thin white cloth
1 pc cellophane

PROCEDURES

1 Wash glutinous rice thoroughly, fill in water until it is slightly above the rice and leave the rice to soak overnight, and then strain. Grind Chinese yeast cake and then divide it into 5 portions.

2 Line white cloth on a steamer, spread glutinous rice on it evenly, and then steam it on high heat for about an hour until cooked.

3 Toss the rice with chopsticks, add in boiling water and mix well, and then steam for another 20 minutes.

4 Put all the rice into a sieve and rinse it with tap water (but not cold boiled water). When rice is loosened, strain it for a short while and then add in ⅘ of fine ground yeast cake immediately and stir thoroughly.

5 Spread the rice gently in a clean clay pot or bowl, and then sprinkle the remaining yeast cake on top. Make a hole in its centre with a rolling pin, and then seal tightly. Place it in a warm area for about 3 to 4 days. When wine seeps into the hole and a fragrant smell comes out, it is ready to serve.

NOTE: Store the wine in a refrigerator for a lasting shelf life.

材 料

糯米1斤（600克）
酒餅1粒
滾水1/4杯
薄白布1塊
玻璃紙1張

做 法

1 糯米洗淨，以過面清水浸過夜，瀝乾。酒餅壓碎分成5份。

2 將濕白布墊在蒸籠內，平均放上糯米，以大火和大滾水蒸約1小時至熟。

3 用筷子翻動，加入滾水拌勻，再蒸約20分鐘。

4 將糯米飯倒在筲箕中，以清水沖淨（不能用冷開水），待飯粒散開，略瀝乾，立即加入4/5酒餅拌勻。

5 把飯輕輕鋪入已清潔的粗硃或瓦煲，把餘下的酒餅灑面，再以輾棍在中間位置開一洞，蓋密，置溫暖處約3-4天。飯洞呈酒液和有香味溢出，即可。

註：如放進冰箱，可持久不變。

客家糯米酒

Hakka-styled Glutinous Rice Wine

時間：2小時
份量：2-3斤
Processing Time: 2 hours
Servings: 1200g - 1800g

INGREDIENTS
1200g glutinous rice
2 Chinese yeast cakes (finely ground)

PROCEDURES
1 Add water to glutinous rice until the water level is slightly above rice and leave it to soak overnight. Wash it thoroughly and then strain slightly.

2 Line a wet white cloth on steamer, put in glutinous rice, and then steam on high heat for about 40 minutes.

3 Place the rice into a sieve, and then rinse with tap water to make it less sticky but warm. Divide the lukewarm glutinous rice and yeast cake into 8 portions.

4 Place one portion of rice in a clean bowl, sprinkle a portion of yeast cake on top, and then some warm water (about 2 tbsp). Repeat this process until all rice and fine ground yeast cake have been put in.

5 Seal the bowl tightly with cloth, cover it with a lid, wrap it with thick clothes or cloth to keep it warm, and then leave it in a warm place unmoved for 7 days to let it brew. You may even leave it for 3 months for more wine. Then filter out the residual fermented glutinous rice, leave it for a longer period, and a golden sweet wine is made.

NOTE: You can buy Chinese yeast cake in Chinese wineries or liquor stores. It is light brown in a round cake shape. Not the ball-like yeast cake which sold in Shanghainese grocery stores.

材 料
糯米2斤（1200克）
酒餅2個（研碎）

做 法
1 米用過面清水浸過夜，洗淨，略為瀝乾。

2 將濕布墊在蒸籠內，放下糯米，以大火蒸熟約40分鐘。

3 把糯米飯倒在隔篩上，略沖（減黏性），仍帶餘溫，並與酒餅均分成8份。

4 將一份糯米飯置已清潔的盆中，灑上一份酒餅，再灑些溫水（約2湯匙），重複至完為止。

5 用布包密盆口，加蓋後置放在溫暖處，以厚衣服或厚布蓋着，保持溫暖，不能移動，待7日成酒。（需要多些酒液，可放置3個月，隔去酒醩，再待些日子便可。）

註：酒餅可在買酒之地方轉讓，顏色及形狀像茶仔，並不是南貨店所售賣的丸狀。

檸檬酒
Lemon Wine

時間：15分鐘
份量：1公升
Processing Time: 15 minutes
Servings: 1 litre

INGREDIENTS

4 lemons
500g Chinese white liquor
220g rock sugar

PROCEDURES

1 Remove the seeds of 2 lemons and then cut into slices.

2 Squeeze out the juice of the remaining 2 lemons. Break the rock sugar into small pieces.

3 Place the lemon slices and juice in a wide-mouth glass bottle, add in rock sugar.

4 Fill in Chinese white liquor slowly, cover the bottle with a cling wrap and a lid securely, leave it for about 1 week to let the rock sugar dissolve, and the wine is made.

NOTE: This lemon wine can be served as a refreshing drink with 7-Up (Sprite) or soda water and ice cubes.

材料

檸檬4個

玉冰燒500克

冰糖5½兩（220克）

做法

1 把2個檸檬去核、切片。

2 餘下2個榨汁；冰糖舂碎。

3 檸檬片放入玻璃瓶中，注入檸檬汁，然後加入冰糖。

4 將玉冰燒慢慢注入，用保鮮紙封住瓶口，加蓋封好，待冰糖自動溶解，約1星期後才可取用。

註：可取適量檸檬酒，再加些七喜或梳打汽水及冰塊飲用，非常可口。

菩提酒

Grape Wine

時間：10分鐘
份量：3公升
Processing Time: 10 minutes
Servings: 3 litres

INGREDIENTS

900g fresh black grapes
450g rock sugar (ground)
9 cups or 2250g cool boiled water

PROCEDURES

1 Wash grapes thoroughly, strain until extremely dry, mash and then put it in a clean glass bottle.

2 Add in rock sugar and fill in cool boiled water until 80% full. Seal the bottle tightly and then store it in a cool place.

3 Leave it for 3 months. If the grapes float, it means fermentation has been completed. You may then filter out the grapes and a luxuriant grape wine is made.

Remarks:

1 You must use cool boiled water for brewing, not the chilled water from the refrigerator.

2 Don't fill in the bottle fully, leaving some room for fermentation.

3 The bottle must be sealed tightly and left unmoved during fermentation or the wine brewed will have a sour taste.

NOTE: The longer the storage period, the better the wine.

材 料

新鮮黑葡萄2磅(900克)
冰糖(打碎)1磅(450克)
凍滾水9杯(2250克)

做 法

1 葡萄洗淨、瀝水至極乾,壓破後放入清潔之玻璃瓶中。

2 加入冰糖及八成滿之凍滾水,將瓶口封密,放陰涼處。

3 待3個月後(約100日),見葡萄浮起,即表示發酵完成,便可將葡萄隔去,即成香醇鮮艷之菩提酒。

注意:

1 釀酒之凍滾水,一定要夠凍,但是不能用雪凍之冰水。

2 玻璃瓶不能裝得太滿,因為要預留空位給葡萄發酵。

3 瓶口必定要封密,時候未到,不能移動及打開,否則酒會有酸味。

註:酒存放時間越久,香味越醇。

欖豉醬

Olive and Black Beans Paste

時間：10分鐘
份量：1500克
Processing Time: 10 minutes
Servings: 1500

材料

材料A

生薑55克

蒜頭100克

豆豉180克

油欖角100克

紫蘇2.5克

生油或粟米油1½杯

材料B

糖130克（先下）

醋30克

生抽125克

蠔油125克

清水125克

材料C

生粉10克

水20克

做法

1 將生薑、蒜頭、豆豉、油欖角和紫蘇洗淨，瀝乾，以攪拌機打碎。

2 燒熱油，加入豆豉混合物，以慢火炒香（約5分鐘）。

3 將B料加入，以慢火煮滾。

4 加入C料推勻即成。

INGREDIENTS

INGREDIENT A

55g raw ginger

100g garlic

180g preserved black beans

100g Chinese salted olives

2.5g perilla

1½ cups cooking oil or corn oil

INGREDIENT B

130g sugar (to be added firstly)

30g vinegar

125g soy sauce

125g oyster sauce

125g water

INGREDIENT C

10g cornstarch

20g water

PROCEDURES

1 Wash ginger, garlic, preserved black beans, Chinese salted olives and perilla thoroughly, strain, and then grind with an electric blender.

2 Heat up oil, add in black bean paste mixture 1, and then stir-fry on low heat for about 5 minutes.

3 Add in ingredient B and cook on low heat until it boils.

4 Add in ingredient C, stir well and ready to use.

自製南乳
Homemade Fermented Red Taro Curd

材 料

白芽芋1斤（600克）

麵粉3兩（120克）

粗鹽3兩（120克）

後下料

生抽1枝（500克）

花紅粉½茶匙

五香粉1茶匙

玫瑰露酒2湯匙

做 法

1 白芽芋洗淨，原個蒸熟去皮，壓成芋泥備用。

2 麵粉加入少許水開成糊狀，蒸熟（約15分鐘），待凍。

3 粗鹽加入適量滾水浸溶待凍。

4 將芋泥、麵糊和鹽水同置大盆中搓透，轉放瓦盆置室內擺放，不用上蓋，任由它發霉（越腐化則越好）。

5 經過15天的時間，轉放在陽光下曬，期間必須每2-3小時，用筷子拌勻1次。

6 把曬好的芋頭混合物傾在盤上，按壓成四方形（如板豆腐），再壓實切件，排放在已用少許玫瑰露酒搪勻的缸內。

7 把"後下料"拌勻，放在芋頭混合物方塊上，密封放置1個月以上，即成。

注意：

① 芋頭分荔甫芋、紅芽芋、白芽芋和檳榔芋等，做南乳必須用白芽芋。

② 沒有瓦缸的話，可改用玻璃瓶。

③ 南乳入缸後淋上生抽香料，貯藏越久則越入味。

INGREDIENTS

600g white taro
120g flour
120g coarse salt

FINAL STAGE INGREDIENTS

500g soy sauce
½ tsp red colour powder
1 tsp five-spice powder
2 tbsp rose wine

PROCEDURES

1 Wash white taro thoroughly, steam until cooked, peel, mash into purée and then set aside.

2 Put flour in a bowl, add in a little water and mix into a batter. Steam for about 15 minutes until cooked and set aside.

3 Dissolve coarse salt in some boiling water and leave to cool.

4 When the above ingredients are cool, put taro purée, batter and salty water together in a mixing bowl and knead well. Transfer the dough to a pottery bowl, uncovered and leave it to ferment at room temperature.

5 Leave it for 15 days and then expose to direct sunlight and toss it with chopsticks every 2 to 3 hours.

6 Pour the dried ingredients into a square tray, press firmly and then cut into pieces. Line the curds orderly in an urn smeared with rose wine on its inner wall.

7 Mix the final stage ingredients thoroughly. Pour it over the taro mixture, leave it for a month and ready to use.

Remarks:

① There are different types of taro but only white taro can be used for making fermented red taro curd.

② If no pottery urn is available, use a glass container instead.

③ After pouring the spicy mixture into the urn of taro curd, leave it for at least one month before use for a better taste.

自製食材
HOMEMADE INGREDIENTS

食材親手做

　　自製食材的意思，是用一些生料加以處理，製成一些食物的原材料。這些食材，可以獨當一面作主角，亦可以做大配角，配合其他用料製作出各式各樣的美食。例如：臘腸、臘肉等便是。既可獨立蒸煮，或可作煲仔飯的主料；但配合其他物料如荷豆、芹菜等，將其切片炒製，便成佐膳佳餚；做糯米飯更是絕配。

　　說起曬臘肉及臘腸，少不免又勾起舊日情懷，回顧少年時舊居，廚房外的吊橋是開放式建築，站在那裏，能看見前後街數十戶的廚房。掛在晾衣架上的，很多時並不是衣服，而是一條條顏色鮮明、油光潤澤的臘製品或醬鯪魚，蔚為奇觀。

　　做臘製品要選秋高氣爽，或乾爽的北風天，臘製品便不會漏油和招惹蒼蠅。以前的樓宇曬晾地方充足，做大量的臘肉時，還可以送到天台上去吸收陽光。現在的住所，很多連曬衣服的地方也不足夠，更別說要曬臘肉了。

　　要親嘗製作的滿足感而不受環境的限制，便要動動腦筋。我們可以把冷氣機調得冷一點，利用冷氣機的冷風和抽濕作用，把肉吹至乾爽。當肉變硬及乾身後，便用保鮮紙個別包好，再放入保鮮袋中封密，然後放雪櫃保存。要注意的是，如果希望物料更乾爽，便不要放在冰格內，冰格並不能把食物收乾，只會保持其水份。

Ingredients DIY

We can make some raw materials into usable ingredients, such as Chinese sausages and dry bacon, for dishes. They can be steamed on their own or as the main ingredients for clay pot rice, cut into slices and stir-fried with vegetables like snow peas and celery, or even be used as a perfect match for glutinous rice.

In the old days, people used to hang Chinese sausages, bacon and fish to dry in kitchens. These dry products were usually made in autumns when the weather was cool and dry, so that they would not drip oil and attract any flies. Some would even expose them to direct sunlight on rooftop if there was one. However, as the living space in Hong Kong is getting smaller and smaller, many people don't have enough hanging place for clothes, not to mention the drying place for sausages and bacon.

Despite the physical constraints encountered, we should be flexible and adaptable to our changing environment. Instead of hanging bacon to dry in an airy place, we may dehumidify it with an air-conditioner until the meat is dry and hard. Then we can wrap it up with cling paper, put it into a zipploc, have it securely sealed and then store it in a refrigerator. But don't put it in a freezer, which will maintain the moisture of food instead of dehydrating it.

自製臘腸

Homemade Chinese Sausages

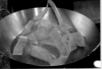

材 料

瘦肉½斤（300克）

肥肉3兩（120克）

腸衣適量

冰肉醃料

糖2湯匙

鹽½茶匙

醃料

糖½茶匙

鹽½茶匙

生抽2½湯匙

老抽½茶匙

玫瑰露酒1兩（40克）

做 法

1　腸衣用清水浸約15分鐘（至軟身），
　　盛起，瀝乾。

2　瘦肉切粒加醃料拌勻，醃過夜。

3　肥肉切幼粒，加冰肉醃料拌勻醃過
　　夜，飛水，過冷，瀝乾。

4　瘦肉和冰肉同放盤中拌勻再醃1小
　　時，即成臘腸餡。

5　將餡料塞滿腸衣內，約5吋長，用
　　繩紮着，再用針插孔。

6　放入大熱水中浸一浸，掛在當風處
　　吹乾。

註：可吹至六、七成乾燥，再以火焙至完
　　全乾透即成。

INGREDIENTS
300g lean pork
120g fatty pork
Some pork intestine skin

MARINADES FOR FATTY PORK
2 tbsp sugar
½ tsp salt

MARINADES
½ tbsp sugar
½ tsp salt
2½ tbsp soy sauce
½ tsp dark soy sauce
40g rose wine

PROCEDURES
1　Soak pork intestine skin in water for
　about 15 minutes until softened and
　then strain.
2　Cut lean pork into fine dices, add in
　marinade, and marinate overnight.
3　Cut fatty pork into fine dices, add
　in fatty pork marinade, leave it
　overnight. Then blanch in hot water,
　rinse with tap water and strain.
4　Put both types of pork in a bowl, mix
　well and leave it to marinate for an
　hour as sausage filling.
5　Stuff the filling into intestine skin to
　make a sausage of about 5 inches
　long, tie it with string and then pierce
　some holes on it with a needle.
6　Soak it in boiling water for a short
　while and then hang in a airy place to
　dry.

NOTE: When the sausages are about 60-70%
　　dry, hang it above fire until completely
　　dry.

自製煙肉

Homemade Smoked Bacon

時間：10分鐘
份量：1斤
Processing time: 10 minutes
Servings: 600g

材料

五花腩肉1斤(600克)

糖2茶匙

錫紙1張

醃料

粗鹽1兩(40克)

花椒(打碎)2茶匙

八角(打碎)2粒

煙燻料

紅茶葉2/3杯

片糖碎1/3杯

做法

1 腩肉去毛洗淨，連皮切約1/2吋厚長條形。

2 花椒、八角樁碎，加入鹽以白鑊炒至呈黃色。

3 加入醃料，用力擦勻，醃2天(期間翻動2-3次)，醃透後以溫水洗淨。

4 再用清水浸15分鐘後，掛起吹乾。

5 將錫紙墊鑊中，放入拌勻之煙燻料，放上鐵架，將吹乾之腩肉排在架上。

6 蓋上鑊蓋，以大火燻約4分鐘，開蓋翻轉1次。

7 合蓋再燻3分鐘，見肉呈金黃色即成。

註：可蒸熟切片吃，或切片加配菜同炒，亦可切薄片，煎熟作早餐。

INGREDIENTS

600g pork belly

2 tsp sugar

1 pc aluminium foil

MARINADES

40g coarse salt

2 tsp Sichuan peppercorn (finely ground)

2 pcs star aniseed (finely ground)

SMOKING INGREDIENTS

2/3 cup black tea leaves

1/3 cup chopped cane sugar

PROCEDURES

1 Remove hair of pork belly, wash thoroughly, and then cut it into long sticks of about 1/2 inch thick with skin intact.

2 Grind Sichuan peppercorn and star aniseed. Add in salt and stir-fry in a dry hot wok until golden brown.

3 Rub the pork hard with the marinade and marinate for 2 days (turn the pork 2 to 3 times in between). Wash the marinated pork with warm water thoroughly.

4 Soak it in water for 15 minutes and then hang to dry.

5 Line aluminium foil on a wok, put mixed smoking ingredients on it, put in an iron rack and then the pork on top.

6 Cover with a lid, smoke it on high heat for about 4 minutes, remove the lid and turn the pork once.

7 Cover it with a lid again and smoke for another 3 minutes until the pork turned golden brown.

NOTE: The smoked bacon can be cooked by steaming and then served in slices. It may also be sliced and then stir-fried with vegetable, or simply pan-fried for breakfast.

自製鹹魚
Homemade Salted Fish

時間：10分鐘
份量：2-3斤
Processing Time: 10 minutes
Servings: 1200g to 1800g

INGREDIENTS

Some croakers
A few catties raw salt

PROCEDURES

1 Remove internal organs of fish, wash thoroughly and then pat dry.
2 Stuff large amount of salt into fish belly and gill.
3 Get a large wooden bucket (or basin). Put in a layer of salt and then some salt-stuffed fish, and repeat this process until all fish are placed. Cover the top with salt.
4 Marinate for 3-5 days. Take out the fish, expose them to direct sunlight by lining in an open area or hanging on rooftop, and let them sunbathe for 2-3 days before use.

NOTE: If the fish are well attended, their meat will become tasty and succulent, otherwise, they will go rotten and stinky. They should only be exposed to sunlight in open air and must be returned to the salt bucket in rainy or cloudy days.

材 料

馬友或黃花魚(任何鹹水魚類均可)數條
生鹽數斤

做 法

1 鮮魚剖好洗淨及抹乾。
2 立即以大量生鹽塞進魚肚和魚腮內。
3 用一個大木桶(或大盤),按序放下生鹽、已塞鹽的魚、生鹽……。如是者至完成,最面層應是鹽蓋頂。
4 醃約3-5天後取出,放在空地或掛在天台曬太陽,曬至2-3日便可食用。

註:這醃法如醃得好就變成梅香鹹魚;若醃得不好,鹹魚便會腐臭。故曬時遇到雨天或陰天,應立即收回鹹魚,回放盤內照舊醃之,待天色晴朗又再復曬。鹹魚要曬得夠乾爽才好吃。

臘肉
Dry Blanched Pork

材料

五花腩肉1斤（600克）
頭遍老抽2湯匙
醬色¼茶匙

醃料（拌勻）
粗鹽1茶匙
醬油¼杯
玫瑰露酒1½湯匙
糖1½湯匙

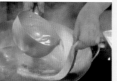

做法

1 豬肉連皮切約½吋厚長條，洗淨瀝乾。

2 醃料拌勻，放入五花腩肉醃10小時。

3 每件豬肉均用繩穿起，放大滾水中飛水。

4 掛在當風處吹，約½天（不能太乾）。

5 老抽和醬色拌勻，加入豬肉拌透（每件豬肉均要沾滿顏色），掛在當風處吹乾。

INGREDIENTS
600g pork belly
2 tbsp supreme dark soy sauce
¼ tsp fine dark soy sauce

MARINADE (STIRRED)
1 tsp coarse salt
¼ cup soy sauce
1½ tsp rose wine
1½ tsp sugar

PROCEDURES

1 Cut pork, with skin intact, into long strips of about ½ inch thick. Wash and strain.

2 Mix Marinade, add in pork and leave to marinate for 10 hours.

3 String the pork and then blanch in boiling water.

4 Hang to dry in an airy place for about ½ day. (don't let it dry out)

5 Mix dark soy sauce with fine dary soy sauce, add in pork and mix until every piece is smeared with sauce evenly. Hang to dry in an airy place.

家鄉風肉
Country Dry-cure Ham

材料
五花腩肉1斤（600克）
粗鹽1¼茶匙

醃料
磨豉醬1¼兩（50克）
糖1茶匙
玫瑰露酒1½湯匙
醬油1湯匙

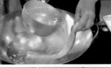

做法

1 豬肉切成長條，像臘肉般大小，用粗鹽擦勻，醃1小時。

2 把醃料拌勻，塗在已醃鹽之豬肉上，置盆中，續醃24小時（使醃料沾滿豬肉）。

3 以繩穿起豬肉，掛在當風處吹乾，約7天（用手按豬肉，如覺硬實，即已乾爽）便可食用。

註：蒸熟切片吃，或配以其他材料燜、炒亦可。

INGREDIENTS
600g pork belly
1¼ tsp coarse salt

MARINADES
50g brown bean paste
1 tsp sugar
1½ tsp rose wine
1 tbsp soy sauce

PROCEDURES

1 Cut pork into long strips like dry blanched pork, rub with coarse salt and marinate for an hour.

2 Mix Marinade and smear on the salted pork. Put in a basin and marinate for 24 hours.

3 String the pork and hang to dry in an airy place for about 7 days. Then check the pork by pressing it with hands. If it is hard, it is dry and ready to use.

NOTE: Slice the ham after being steamed. Another suggestion that you can accompany with other sub-ingredients for stewing and stir-frying.

醬油仁梒

Renmen Berry in Soy Sauce

時間：15分鐘
份量：1斤
Processing time: 15 minutes
Serving: 600g

INGREDIENTS

600g renmen berries
2 tbsp coarse salt
1 bottle soy sauce
¼ cup vinegar for preserved ginger
  (optional)
100g brown sugar

PROCEDURES

1 Wear gloves, mix berries and salt
  with hands for about 5 minutes until
  colour changes. Then wash and strain.

2 Boil sugar in soy sauce until it
  dissolves, leave it to cool, and then
  add in ¼ cup of vinegar.

3 Crack berries, line them in a bottle,
  pour in soy sauce mixture, and then
  leave for at least a week. Ready to
  serve.

材 料

仁稔1斤（600克）

粗鹽2湯匙

醬油1枝

醃酸薑醋（隨意）1/4杯

黃砂糖100克

做 法

1 戴上手套，用粗鹽揉捏仁稔，揉捏
  至變色（約需5分鐘），洗淨瀝乾。

2 將糖加入醬油煮溶，攤凍，加1/4杯
  醋。

3 將仁稔敲裂，排放入樽，然後倒入
  醬油料，最少放置一星期，可吃。

調味醬料的佳餚
DISHES WITH HOMEMADE INGREDIENTS AND SAUCES

自製材料的合併運用

此部份是教大家如何利用製成的配料，可合併其他物料做菜。這裏有個很好的代表作"秘製鹹香骨"，便用上了自家醃製的鹹魚，配合腐乳和肋排做成。用鹹魚醃肉，有增香效果；腐乳則有發酵作用，使肉骨鬆軟，無需使用梳打粉、鬆肉粉等東西，亦能做到外脆內軟的質感。

如棄腐乳改用南乳，質感相同，味道略濃但相近，兩者皆可口，更兼同時採用兩款自製食材配合製成菜餚，成功感更甚，如何選擇應用，任隨喜好。

近年經科學研究，認為吃鹹魚容易致癌，建議人們少吃。但舊社會的長輩，尤其是鄉間的先祖們，皆相信多食鹽才會有力，因此鹹魚成為家家必備的食糧，鹹魚煮粥仔，更是味美非凡的育兒良方。每個人對健康的看法及常識，都有不同智慧和見解。在此，我不會把鹹魚特別推薦給大家，但鹹魚食製的鍾愛感情，在我個人而言，仍然濃烈。

荷芹炒臘肉或臘味，是歲晚新年的家常菜式，加入芽菇，更添鄉土之情。市面醃漬的仁稔，以酸甜居多。用自家製作的醬油醃法，做出來的仁稔，風味與別不同，配合油渣蒸製的斑頭腩，有上佳的評價。

特別推介的酒釀豬肚，其可口之處，教人一試難忘。可惜的是，我至今仍未能在本港的食肆中品嚐得到。此菜要做得好，選酒要上乘，糯米酒的顏色與香氣，以陳年為佳。荔枝與龍眼的味道清甜，以用鮮品為上選，乾貨與罐頭的品質及食味都相差太遠。但是一旦鮮果如非當造，我建議用罐裝的總比乾貨的好，雖然不如理想，效果也達標準。

DIY Ingredients Combo

In this section, we are going to make dishes using the self-made ingredients introduced in the previous sections. A good representation of it is "tasty spare ribs", which is made of homemade salted fish, fermented bean curds and spare ribs. Salted fish is aromatic while fermented taro curds can tenderize meat and bones.

You may replace fermented bean curds with fermented red bean curds for a stronger taste of the latter. I am sure it will give you great satisfaction if you can mix and match the ingredients made by yourself.

In recent years, it is found that salted fish may induce cancer and thus, not recommended. But in the past, Chinese people, especially those living in villages, believed that salt could give us energy and salted fish was an essential household food. It was even added to the congee for young children. Having grown up with this delicacy, I still have a special affection for it despite the resentment from the medical world due to health reasons.

Stir-fried dry bacon with snow peas and celery is a popular dish for family dinners around Chinese New Year. We can add an extra touch of Nostalgia for country dishes by putting in some arrow heads.

The pickled Renmen available is usually sweet and sour in taste. In this book, I introduce a different flavour, Renmen in soy sauce, which is a good complement for steamed fish head.

Last but not the least, I strongly recommend my favourite "braised pig abdomen in wine", which is not provided by the restaurants in Hong Kong. To make it well, you must select an aged glutinous rice wine of high quality, and fresh Lychees and Longans for their refreshing taste. However, if the fruits are not in season, you can replace them with canned fruits, but not the dried ones.

糯米酒醩雞

Braised Chicken with Fermented Glutinous Rice

時間：15分鐘
份量：2-4人
Processing time: 15 minute
Serving: 2-4 person

INGREDIENTS

½ dressed chicken
40g ginger (chopped)
¼ cup glutinous rice wine
3 tbsp fermented glutinous rice

MARINADES

1 tsp cornstarch
1 tbsp cooked oil
1 tbsp glutinous rice wine

SEASONINGS

¼ cup water
1 tbsp brown sugar

材料

雞½隻
薑（剁碎）1兩（40克）
糯米酒¼杯
酒醋3湯匙

醃料
生粉1茶匙
熟油1湯匙
糯米酒1湯匙

調味料
清水¼杯
黃砂糖1湯匙

PROCEDURES

1 Chop chicken into pieces, add in marinade and mix well.
2 Leave it for 15 minutes. Blanch it in hot oil.
3 Heat some oil and stir-fry chopped ginger in it.
4 Return chicken to a wok, add in glutinous rice wine, fermented glutinous rice and seasoning.
5 When it is boiling, lower the heat to medium or low and cook for another 10 minutes. Ready to serve.

NOTE: Use wine to cook food that no need add salt in the dishes. Otherwise, its flavour will turn to sour and bad taste.

做法

1 雞斬件加醃料拌勻。
2 15分鐘後泡油。
3 燒熱適量油，爆香薑碎。
4 雞件回鑊拌勻，放下糯米酒、酒醋及調味。
5 沸滾後，改以中慢火煮10分鐘即成。

註：用酒煮物，不用下鹽，否則變酸不好吃。

秘製鹹香骨
Tasty Spare-ribs

時間：20分鐘
份量：4-6人
Processing time: 20 minutes
Serving: 4-6 persons

INGREDIENTS

600g spare-ribs
20g salted croaker
1 fermented bean curb
1 tbsp minced ginger
Some cornstarch

MARINADES

1 tbsp soy sauce
1 tbsp oyster sauce
1½ tsp sugar
1 egg yolk
1 tsp ginger juice
1 tsp Shaoxing wine
2 tbsp cornstarch

材 料

豬肋排1斤（600克）
馬友鹹魚½兩（20克）
腐乳1件
薑蓉1湯匙
生粉適量

PROCEDURES

1 Chop ribs into pieces. Debone salted croaker and mince the fish meat.
2 Mix ribs, fish minced and marinade in a basin, and marinate for an hour.
3 Coat with cornstarch.
4 Deep-fry it in medium-hot oil for about 6 minutes until golden brown. Strain off excess oil and serve.

醃料

醬油1湯匙
蠔油1湯匙
糖1½茶匙
蛋黃1隻
薑汁1茶匙
紹酒1茶匙
生粉2湯匙

做 法

1 肋排斬件，馬友鹹魚起肉剁蓉。
2 將排骨、鹹魚蓉及醃料置盤中拌匀，醃1小時。
3 撲上乾生粉。
4 放八成熱油中，炸至金黃熟透（約6分鐘）即可，盛起瀝油上碟即成。

荷芹炒臘肉

Stir-fried Dry Bacon with Snow Peas and Chinese Celery

時間：5-8分鐘
份量：4-6人
Processing time: 5-8 minutes
Serving: 4-6 persons

INGREDIENTS

120g dry blanched pork (slices)
  (refer to p.30)
80g snow peas
80g Chinese celery
80g leek
6 slices carrot
4 slices ginger

SEASONINGS

Some sesame oil
1 tbsp oyster sauce
1 tsp soy sauce
¼ tsp sugar
¼ tsp salt
1 tsp cornstarch
4 tbsp water

PROCEDURES

1　Cut dry blanched pork into slices.
2　Wash snow peas, Chinese celery and leek, and then cut them up.
3　Add a little oil to a hot wok, add in the dry blanched pork, ginger and sub-ingredients, and stir-fry thoroughly on high heat.
4　Stir in seasonings and mix well. Ready to serve.

材 料

臘肉（切片）3兩（120克）（參考30頁）
荷蘭豆2兩（80克）
芹菜2兩（80克）
大蒜2兩（80克）
甘筍花6片
薑花4片

調味
麻油少許
蠔油1湯匙
醬油1茶匙
糖¼茶匙
鹽¼茶匙
生粉1茶匙
水4湯匙

做 法

1　臘肉切片。
2　荷豆、芹菜、大蒜洗淨，摘好。
3　熱鑊下油少許，爆香臘肉、薑花及配菜，以大火炒透。
4　加調味拌勻上碟。

麵醬油渣仁棯蒸頭腩

Steamed Fish Head and Belly with Brown Bean Paste

時間：10-15分鐘
份量：4-6人
Processing time: 10-15 minutes
Serving: 4-6 persons

INGREDIENTS
400g fish head and belly (any fish)
40g brown bean paste
40g renmen berries (preserved, refer to p.33)
60g deep-fried pork belly crisps
10g dried tangerine peel (soaked and shredded)
10g garlic
some spring onion (shredded)

SEASONING
Some soy sauce

PROCEDURES
1 Wash fish head and belly and put it in a plate.
2 Mix brown bean paste, dried tangerine peel, minced garlic, renmen berries, pork crisps and fish head together.
3 Place the dish into a steamer and steam on high heat for about 8 minutes. Take it out, scoop out the liquid, and then sprinkle shredded spring onion on top.
4 Heat up 2-3 tbsp oil, pour it over the fish, and then pour in seasoning. Ready to serve.

材 料
任何魚類頭腩400克
磨豉醬40克
仁梣(醃製)40克(參閱第33頁)
豬油渣60克
陳皮(浸透切絲)10克
蒜肉10克
葱絲少許

調味
醬油適量

做 法
1 頭腩洗淨置碟中。
2 磨豉醬、陳皮、蒜蓉、仁梣及豬油渣與頭腩拌勻。
3 置蒸籠,以大火蒸約8分鐘,取出潷去汁水,灑上葱絲。
4 煮2-3湯匙油,潷於葱絲上面,淋上調味即成。

脆貝豉蒜燜苦瓜

Braised Dried Scallops with Bitter Melon

時間：15分鐘
份量：4-6人
Processing time: 15 minutes
Serving: 4-6 persons

INGREDIENTS

40g dried scallops
600g bitter melon
10g preserved black beans
10g minced garlic

SEASONINGS

1 tsp soy sauce
1 tbsp oyster sauce
Some sesame oil
Some pepper
1 tsp cornstarch
4 tbsp water

PROCEDURES

1 Soak dried scallops, shred and then deep-fry to crispy. Set aside.

2 Cut bitter melon into slices, blanch in hot water and then strain.

3 Heat up 2 tbsp of oil, stir-fry preserved black beans, put in bitter melon and stir-fry thoroughly.

4 Stir in seasonings, dish, and then sprinkle crispy scallop on top. Ready to serve.

材　料
瑤柱40克
涼瓜600克
豆豉10克
蒜蓉10克

調味
醬油1茶匙
蠔油1湯匙
麻油少許
胡椒粉少許
生粉1茶匙
水4湯匙

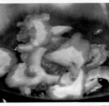

做 法

1 瑤柱浸透撕開，炸脆備用。

2 涼瓜切片，飛水瀝乾。

3 燒油2湯匙，爆香豉蒜，傾下涼瓜炒透。

4 調味拌勻上碟，灑上炸脆瑤柱。

酒釀窩蛋

Egg in Glutinous Rice Wine

時間：10分鐘
份量：4-6人
Processing time: 10 minutes
Serving: 4-6 persons

INGREDIENTS
4 cups water
150g rock sugar
3 tbsp glutinous rice wine (refer to p.11)
1 egg (beaten)
4 eggs

THICKENING SAUCES
4 tbsp water chestnut powder
5 tbsp water

PROCEDURES
1 Pour water into a pot, add in rock sugar and cook until sugar dissolves.
2 Mix thickening sauce, add into sweet soup and mix into a porridge, pour in glutinous rice wine, stir well and then turn off the heat.
3 Beat an egg thoroughly and then stir into the porridge.
4 Break 4 eggs into the soup one by one and a refreshing and tasty sweet is ready to serve.

材　料
清水4杯
冰糖4兩（150克）
酒釀3湯匙（參閱第11頁）
蛋液1隻
雞蛋4隻

芡料
馬蹄粉4湯匙
水5湯匙

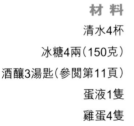

做　法
1 清水注入鍋中，加冰糖煮溶。
2 芡料調勻，加入糖水中，拌勻成馬蹄糊，再將酒釀倒下，拌勻熄火。
3 把1隻蛋打成蛋液，加在馬蹄糊中拌成蛋花。
4 最後將4隻雞蛋，逐一打入，便成一款清熱可口的甜品。

家鄉風肉百頁結

Country Dry-cure Ham with Shanghainese Bean Curd Knots

時間：20分鐘
份量：4-6人
Processing time: 20 minutes
Serving: 4-6 persons

INGREDIENTS
80g country dry cure ham (refer to p.31)
80g Shanghainese bean curd knots
150g Beijing cabbage
8 slices carrot
2 slices ginger
2 cups broth

SEASONING
Some salt

PROCEDURES
1 Wash country dry cure ham and cut into slices.
2 Blanch bean curd knots in hot water with soda powder, rinse with tap water, and then strain.
3 Heat up a little oil, stir in ginger, and then pour in broth.
4 Add in the ham, bean curd sheet knots, Beijing cabbage and carrot slices.
5 Cook for about 15 minutes, add salt to taste and ready to serve.

材 料
家鄉風肉2兩（80克）（參閱第31頁）
百頁結2兩（80克）
娃娃菜4兩（150克）
甘筍花8片
薑2片
上湯2杯

調味
鹽適量

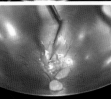

做 法
1 家鄉風肉洗淨，切塊。
2 百頁結用少許梳打粉飛水，過冷，瀝乾。
3 燒少許油，爆香薑片，注入上湯。
4 加入家鄉風肉、百頁結、娃娃菜及甘筍。
5 煮約15分鐘，加鹽調味上桌。

欖豉醬蒸金鼓

Steamed Scat with Olive and Black Bean Paste

INGREDIENTS

2 scat fish
2 tbsp olive and black bean paste
 (refer to p.19)
Some shredded spring onion

SEASONING

Some soy sauce

PROCEDURES

1 Wash scat and put in a plate.

2 Smear some olive and black bean paste.

3 Place it into a steamer and steam on high heat for 8 minutes. Take it out and scoop out the liquid.

4 Place shredded spring onion on the fish, and then pour hot oil and soy sauce on top. Ready to serve.

材 料

金鼓魚2條
欖豉醬2湯匙(參閱第19頁)
蔥絲適量

調味
醬油適量

做 法

1 金鼓魚洗淨,置碟中。

2 塗上欖豉醬。

3 置蒸籠以大火蒸8分鐘即可取出,
   漖去汁水。

4 把蔥絲放魚面,灒下滾油及醬油即
   成。

酒釀豬肚

Braised Pig Abdomen with Glutinous Rice Wine

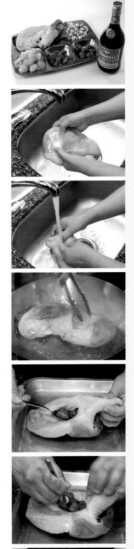

INGREDIENTS

1 pig abdomen
8 red dates (cored)
8 lychees (fresh or canned)
8 longans (fresh or canned)
8 arrow heads (skinned, can be replaced
   with chestnuts)
60g white lotus seeds (boiled for 10
   minutes)
320g glutinous rice wine
Some coriander
1 cup broth

PROCEDURES

1　Remove the fat of pig abdomen, turn it over and scrape the slime off the skin. Rub with cornstarch, salt and cooking oil several times, and then wash thoroughly.

2　Blanch it in boiling water, rinse with tap water and then strain.

3　Stuff all ingredients into the abdomen, and then seal its opening tightly by sewing with a thread. Place it into a basin, pour in 1 cup of broth and then glutinous rice wine. Put it into a steamer and steam for about 3 hours.

4　Take it out, cut off the thread, and take out the stuffing. Transfer it to another dish. Cut the abdomen into slices, lay them orderly on a plate, sprinkle with coriander, pour broth over and serve.

NOTE: This specialty is suitable for Chinese New Year dinners for both family and friends.

材 料

豬肚1個

紅棗（去核）8粒

荔枝（可用罐頭）8粒

桂圓（可用罐頭）8粒

慈菇（可用栗子代替）8粒（刮去皮）

白蓮子60克（用水煮10分鐘）

糯米酒320克

芫荽適量

上湯1杯

做 法

1　豬肚去油，反轉另一面，用刀刮去潺，再以生粉、鹽及生油擦多次，沖洗乾淨。

2　放滾水中飛水，過冷瀝乾。

3　把各配料灌入肚內縫緊，放大碗中，淋1杯上湯加入糯米酒，放蒸籠內，蒸約3小時。

4　取出豬肚拆線後，取出肚中物，另裝盤內，豬肚切片，平鋪其上，灑些芫荽，淋上湯汁，即可上桌。

註 : 酒釀豬肚，風味獨特，無與倫比，春節期間自用和宴客兩相宜。

醋溜骨香魚

Braised Fish Fillet with Fermented Glutinous Rice

材料

桂花魚（起肉斬骨）1條（2斤）1200克

雲耳（浸軟，飛水）少許

生粉適量，青豆40克

醃料A

醬油1湯匙，生粉1湯匙，蛋黃1隻

醃料B

鹽1/4茶匙，生粉1/2茶匙，蛋白1湯匙

薑汁1茶匙，白酒1湯匙

胡椒粉少許，熟油1湯匙

起鑊醬料

薑米2茶匙，蒜蓉2茶匙

辣椒仔（切粒）1隻，豆瓣醬2茶匙

芡汁

酒釀（只要汁）12湯匙（參閱第11頁）

白酒2湯匙，鎮江醋2茶匙，茄汁4湯匙

紅油1/2茶匙，醬油2茶匙，雞粉2茶匙

糖2茶匙，生粉2茶匙

做法

1 桂花魚洗淨，先斬出魚頭及魚尾備用。

2 將魚放平，魚背開始起骨，取出魚肉及魚腩。

3 魚骨斬件，魚肉切厚片，分別用醃料醃15分鐘。

4 先將魚骨、魚頭及魚尾上粉，放油中炸至金黃色，瀝油後置碟中。

5 魚肉泡油至熟，再將魚肉放在魚骨上。

6 燒熱鑊加油，放入鑊醬料炒香，倒入芡汁料煮至濃稠，淋上魚肉上即成。

INGREDIENTS

1200g grouper (deboned)

Some cloud fungus (soaked and then blanched in hot water)

Some cornstarch, 40g green peas

MARINADE A

1 tbsp soy sauce, 1 tbsp cornstarch, 1 egg yolk

MARINADE B

¼ tsp salt, ½ tsp cornstarch

1 tbsp egg white, 1 tsp ginger juice

1 tsp white wine, Some pepper

1 tbsp cooked oil, 2 tsp ginger (finely diced)

START-UP SAUCE INGREDIENTS

2 tsp ginger, 2 tsp minced garlic

1 chili (diced), 2 tsp chili bean sauce

THICKENING SAUCE

12 tbsp glutinous rice wine (refer to p.11)

2 tbsp white wine, 2 tsp dark vinegar

4 tbsp tomato sauce, ½ tsp chili oil

2 tsp soy sauce, 2 tsp chicken powder

2 tsp sugar, 2 tsp cornstarch

PROCEDURES

1 Wash grouper, cut off its head and tail, and set aside.

2 Place it on a table, remove bone from its back, take out fillet and belly.

3 Chop the bone into pieces, cut fillet into thick slices, and marinate them separately with Marinade for 15 minutes.

4 Coat fish bones, head and tail with cornstarch, deep-fry them in oil until golden brown, strain off excess oil and put on a plate.

5 Deep-fry fish fillet until cooked, put it on top of the bones.

6 Add oil to a heated wok, put in start-up sauce ingredients and stir-fry. Pour in thickening sauce and cook until thickened. Pour it over fish fillet. Ready to serve.

懷舊風味私房菜
NOSTALGIC DISHES IN MY KITCHEN

昔日美味今日重現

　　此書撰寫的菜譜，並不是甚麼嶄新創作，大部份都是昔日情懷。儘管沒有創新字眼來包裝和形容我的私房菜譜，但在整體菜單的設計上，從餐前小吃，例如：魚皮花生、麻辣花生；前、主菜的桂花燒腸、燒鴨等。以至單尾的甜品和飯麵，我都一絲不苟把最值得保存的昔日風味重現。

　　其獨特之處，在於很多菜式都是從零開始，由基本的調味、醬料及食材，都由自己親力親為，不假外求。一層層的創造、演變、配合，直至完成整個菜餚，一個掌廚人內心累積的喜悅與豐足，是買現貨回來兜兜炒炒所不能媲美的。

Old Taste New Dishes

Most of the recipes in this book are recalling the taste of old dishes. I have not used any innovative or catchy wordings to package it. Every dish is carefully thought-out and prepared. It contains a full-course menu, including appertizers like crispy peanuts and spicy peanuts; main course like roasted sausages with sweet osmanthus and roasted duck; as well as desserts, rice and noodles, at the end.

The unique feature of my recipes is that I make most of the dishes from ground zero, for instance, making my own seasoning, sauces and ingredients, and then create different delicacies by mix-and-match. Such pleasure and satisfaction can hardly be attained by using readily made products.

魚皮花生
Crispy Peanuts

時間：1小時
份量：1斤
Processing: 1 hour
Serving: 600g

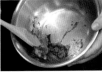

INGREDIENTS

600g peanuts (shelled)
1 pc fermented red trao curd (mashed)
5 pcs garlic (minced)
20g salt

COATING INGREDIENTS

150g flour
1 tsp fine dark soy sauce
Some water

材料

花生肉1斤（600克）
南乳（壓爛）1件
蒜頭（剁蓉）5粒
鹽20克

皮料
麵粉4兩（150克）
醬色（珠油）1茶匙
清水適量

PROCEDURES

1　Put fermented red taro curd and garlic into a wok, add in some oil and stir-fry. Fill in some water (water to peanut ratio is 1:1) and add in salt and peanuts to cook on low heat for an hour.

2　Put cooked peanuts into a sieve, expose to direct sunlight until dried, and set aside.

3　Put flour in a bowl, add in some water and fine dark soy sauce, and mix into a dough.

4　Wrap peanuts with a few dough individually into balls, and then roll on flour.

5　Heat up some oil in a wok until medium hot, put in peanuts and deep-fry until golden brown. Ready to serve.

做法

1　南乳和蒜頭放鑊中，加入少許油爆香，注入適量清水（清水與花生肉份量相若），再加鹽和花生以慢火滾1小時。

2　將已煮好之花生肉傾出，轉放箕盛着，放日光下曬至乾身備用。

3　麵粉放碗中，加入適量清水及醬色拌勻（注意：濃稠度要適中）成糰狀。

4　以麵糰包裹花生肉，搓成一粒粒，再滾上乾麵粉，務使每粒能獨立分開。

5　鑊中放下適量油，燒至八成熱，放下花生，炸至金黃色為標準。

麻辣花生
Hot and Spicy Peanuts

INGREDIENTS

300g peanuts (shelled and skinned)
10g Sichuan peppercorn
20g dried chili
3 star aniseeds
2 tsp spicy chili salt

SEASONINGS

2 cups (500g) water
4 tbsp sugar

PROCEDURES

1 Wash peanuts, put in a pot, add in seasoning and mix well. Cook on medium heat for 9 minutes until water reduced.
2 Take it out, strain and then place in an airy place to dry.
3 Slightly heat up a large amount of oil, add in peppercorn, dried chili, star aniseeds. Then deep-fry peanuts in it until golden brown and float on surface. Take out the peanuts and strain off excess oil.
4 Sprinkle spicy chili salt on peanuts and mix well. Ready to serve.

材 料

花生仁½斤（300克）
花椒粒¼兩（10克）
辣椒乾½兩（20克）
八角3粒
味椒鹽2茶匙

調味
清水2杯（500克）
糖4湯匙

做 法

1 花生仁洗淨放鍋中，加入調味拌勻，以中火煮9分鐘至汁水收乾。
2 盛起、瀝清水份，放當風處吹乾。
3 燒大量油至微溫，放下花椒、辣椒乾、八角及花生炸至浮起呈金黃色盛起，瀝油。
4 將味椒鹽灑花生上拌勻即成。

醬燒鴨下巴

Roasted Duck Jaws

時間：40分鐘
份量：6-8人
Processing time: 40 minutes
Serving: 6-8 person

材料

鴨下巴24隻

薑2片

乾葱4粒

八角4粒

陳皮1角

玫瑰露酒1湯匙

水適量

醬料

麻醬2湯匙

海鮮醬2湯匙

豆瓣醬1½湯匙

柱侯醬½湯匙

五香粉¼茶匙

調味

蠔油½湯匙

醬油1湯匙

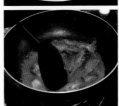

做法

1 鴨下巴洗淨、飛水，用老抽上色，
   瀝乾後泡油備用。

2 燒油2湯匙，爆香薑、乾葱、八
   角、陳皮及醬料，加入鴨下巴炒
   透。

3 注入過面清水，以中慢火燜30分鐘
   至汁液濃稠，盛起，瀝去汁水。

4 將鴨下巴放入焗爐中，以200℃焗
   8分鐘，即成。

INGREDIENTS

24 duck jaws
2 slices ginger
4 shallots
4 star aniseeds
1 dried tangerine peel
1 tbsp rose wine
Some water

SAUCE INGREDIENTS

2 tbsp sesame paste
2 tbsp hoisin sauce
1½ tbsp broad bean sauce
½ tbsp chuhou sauce
¼ tsp five-spice powder

SEASONINGS

½ tbsp oyster sauce
1 tbsp soy sauce

PROCEDURES

1 Wash duck jaws, blanch in hot water,
   and then mix with dark soy sauce.
   Strain and then blanch in hot oil. Set
   aside.

2 Heat up 2 tbsp of oil, stir in ginger,
   shallot, star aniseeds, dried tangerine
   and sauce ingredients, add in duck
   jaws and stir-fry.

3 Fill in some water until it is slightly
   above the ingredients. Stew on
   medium to low heat for 30 minutes
   until the sauce thickens. Take it out
   and strain off excess liquid.

4 Bake duck jaws in an oven at 200℃
   for 8 minutes. Ready to serve.

桂花燒腸

Fragrant Roasted Sausages

時間：30分鐘
份量：6-8件
Processing time: 30 minute.
Serving: 6-8 piece.

材料

腸衣適量，枚頭瘦肉4兩（150克）

豬肝4兩（160克），肥肉3兩（120克）

橙紅色水⅓杯

（橙紅色粉¼茶匙＋清水⅓杯）

醃肥肉料

糖1½湯匙

醃豬肝料

薑汁酒1½湯匙

麥芽糖水

麥芽糖4湯匙，水3湯匙

調味

乾葱蓉2湯匙，蒜蓉2茶匙

沙薑粉1茶匙，麻醬1湯匙

磨豉醬1湯匙，海鮮醬1湯匙

醬油1茶匙，雞粉1茶匙

糖1茶匙，玫瑰露酒2茶匙

做 法

1 腸衣用溫水浸至軟身，清洗內外，瀝乾備用。

2 豬肝切小粒，以醃料拌勻。

3 肥肉切小粒，拌入醃肥肉料，約6小時後，飛水、過冷、瀝乾。

4 瘦肉切小粒，與豬肝、肥肉粒等同置盤中，加入調味撈勻。

5 用漏斗將肉粒塞進腸衣內，頭尾紮緊，在腸衣打孔，略氽水盛起，浸入色粉水上色。

6 把燒腸排在架上，放進已預熱之焗爐中，用200℃焗約20分鐘取出（每隔10分鐘翻轉1次）。

7 把燒腸浸在麥芽糖水中，待沾滿汁液，送回焗爐中焗至兩面皆有少許焦黃。

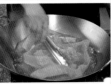

INGREDIENTS

Some pork intestine skin
150g lean pork
160g pig liver
120g fatty pork
⅓ cup orange liquid (¼ tsp orange colouring + ⅓ cup water)

FATTY PORK MARINADE INGREDIENT
1½ tbsp sugar

PIG LIVER MARINADE INGREDIENT
1½ tbsp wine ginger juice

MALTOSE LIQUID
4 tbsp maltose
3 tbsp water

SEASONINGS
2 tbsp dried shallot (minced)
2 tsp minced garlic
1 tsp spicy ginger powder
1 tbsp sesame paste
1 tbsp brown bean paste
1 tbsp hoisin sauce
1 tsp soy sauce
1 tsp chicken powder
1 tsp sugar
2 tsp rose wine

PROCEDURES

1 Soak pork intestine in warm water until softened, wash it inside out, strain and then set aside.

2 Cut pig liver into small dices and then mix with marinade.

3 Cut fatty pork into small dices, mix with fatty pork marinade, leave it for 6 hours, blanch in hot water, rinse with tap water and then strain.

4 Cut lean pork into small dices. Put lean pork, fatty pork and liver into a basin, add in seasoning and mix well.

5 Stuff meat dices into goat intestine with a funnel. Close its end tightly with a string, pierce some holes on it, dip in water for a short while, and then soak in orange liquid for colouring.

6 Place sausages on a rack, bake it in a preheated oven at 200℃ for about 20 minutes and then take it out. (turn sausages every 10 minutes)

7 Soak baked sausages in maltose liquid, return them to oven and bake until golden brown.

涼皮寶玉手撕雞

Shredded Chicken with Green Beans Starch Sheet

時間：50分鐘
份量：10-12人
Processing time: 50 minutes
Serving: 10-12 persons

材料

光雞1隻2斤（1200克）

八角2粒

薑2片

葱2條

粉皮100克

三色椒（切絲）各½隻

木耳（浸透切絲）10克

醃料

玫瑰露酒1湯匙

醬油1湯匙

鹽1湯匙

沙薑粉1茶匙

調味

雞醬¼杯

麻油3湯匙

雞粉1茶匙

魚露1湯匙

蒜蓉1茶匙

做法

1 雞去肺洗淨，以醃料抹勻雞身內外，再將八角、薑、葱放入雞肚中。

2 放入已預熱之焗爐內，以200℃焗45分鐘（中途要翻轉塗油，重複做2次）。

3 焗至金黃取出待凍，拆出雞絲備用。

4 粉皮浸透，放沸水中煮至透明（約5分鐘）。

5 取出粉皮過冷瀝乾，加入三色椒絲及木耳絲。

6 倒下調味拌勻，放碟中，將雞絲放面上即成。

INGREDIENTS

1 dressed whole chicken (1200g)

2 star aniseeds

2 slices ginger

2 sprigs spring onion

100g dried green beans starch sheet

½ red bell pepper, ½ yellow bell pepper and ½ green bell pepper (shredded)

10g wooden fungus (soaked and shredded)

MARINADES

1 tbsp rose wine

1 tbsp soy sauce

1 tbsp salt

1 tsp spicy ginger powder

SEASONINGS

¼ cup Thai chicken paste

3 tbsp sesame oil

1 tsp chicken powder

1 tbsp fish sauce

1 tsp minced garlic

PROCEDURES

1 Remove lungs of chicken, smear its inner and outer walls with marinades, and then stuff star aniseeds, ginger and spring onion into its body.

2 Roast the chicken in an oven at 200℃ for 45 minutes (turn it over 2 times during baking).

3 When it is golden brown, take it out and leave to cool. Then tear its meat into shreds and set aside.

4 Soak green beans starch sheets in water, and then cook it in boiling water for about 5 minutes until it turns translucent.

5 Rinse green beans starch sheets with tap water, strain and shred, and then add in bell peppers and wooden fungus.

6 Mix green beans starch shreds with seasoning and then dish. Put chicken shreds on top. Ready to serve.

涼拌芥辣雞

Chicken and Cucumber with Mustard Oil

時間：25分鐘
份量：6-8人
Processing time: 25 minute
Serving: 6-8 person.

材 料

光雞1隻（約1500克）
青瓜1條

鹵水料

瑞士汁1枝
水4杯

調味汁

醬油4湯匙
鎮江香醋6湯匙
黃砂糖2湯匙
麻油1湯匙
日本青芥醬1湯匙
麻辣油1/2湯匙
上湯2湯匙
生蒜蓉1湯匙
雞粉1茶匙

做 法

1 鹵水料煮沸，放下雞浸20分鐘。

2 取出待凍，斬件。

3 調味拌勻。

4 青瓜切角。

5 將調味淋在雞件及青瓜上，灑上生
   蒜即成。

註：上湯可改用1湯匙雞汁加2湯匙冰水調
    勻。

INGREDIENTS
1 dressed whole chicken (about 1500g)
1 cucumber

SPICY SAUCE INGREDIENTS
1 Swiss sauce
4 cups water

SEASONING SAUCES
4 tbsp soy sauce
6 tbsp dark vinegar
2 tbsp brown sugar
1 tbsp sesame oil
1 tbsp wasabi paste
½ tbsp chili oil
2 tbsp broth
1 tbsp minced garlic
1 tsp chicken powder

PROCEDURES

1 Bring spicy sauce to a boil, put in
   chicken to soak for 20 minutes.

2 Take it out, leave it to cool and then
   chop into pieces.

3 Mix seasoning ingredients well.

4 Cut cucumber into wedges.

5 Pour seasoning over chicken and
   cucumber wedges, and then sprinkle
   raw minced garlic on top. Ready to
   serve.

NOTE: Broth can be replaced with a mixture of
    1 tbsp of chicken soup and 2 tbsp of icy
    water.

燒鴨
Roasted Duck

時間：1.5小時
份量：10-12人
Processing time: 1.5 hours
Serving: 10-12 persons

材 料
光米鴨1隻（約3斤）
薑2片
乾葱頭2個

上皮料
麥芽糖1茶匙
白醋2½湯匙
玫瑰露1茶匙

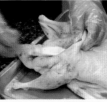

醃料
鹽3茶匙
五香粉1茶匙
八角3粒

做 法

1 白鍋炒醃料。上皮料用熱水坐溶。

2 鴨去肺、洗淨、抹乾，再把醃料放鴨肚內塗勻，放薑片及乾葱，以針縫密。

3 將鴨放沸滾水中拖水，盛起抹乾，把上皮料塗勻鴨皮，置當風處吊乾。

4 預熱焗爐250℃（約15分鐘），將鴨胸向上放在爐架上，離爐頂約2吋位置。

5 焗至金黃色（約30分鐘），改用200℃火焗30分鐘，最後再以250℃火焗15分鐘即成。

註： 注意焗時每15分鐘要翻動位置，使火力均勻。

INGREDIENTS
1 dressed whole duck (about 1800g)
2 slices ginger
2 dried shallot

GLAZING INGREDIENTS
1 tsp maltose
2½ tbsp white vinegar
1 tsp rose wine

MARINADES
3 tsp salt
1 tsp five-spice powder
3 star aniseeds

PROCEDURES

1 Stir-fry marinades in a dry wok. Dissolve glazing ingredients above hot water.

2 Remove the lung of duck, wash and pat dry. Smear Marinade on the inner wall of duck abdomen, put in ginger and shallot, and seal the opening by sewing with a thread.

3 Blanch the duck in boiling water for a short while, take it out and pat dry. Brush glazing ingredients on its skin and then hang in an airy place to dry.

4 Preheat an oven to 250℃ for about 15 minutes. Place the duck on the baking rack and leave about 2-inch spacing between the oven top and the duck.

5 Bake for about 30 minutes. When it turns golden brown, lower heat to 200℃ and bake for another 30 minutes. Then increase the heat to 250℃ and bake for 15 minutes. Ready to serve.

NOTE: Turn the duck every 15 minutes during baking.

陳皮紹酒焗乳鴿

Stewed Baby Pigeons with Shaoxing Wine and Dried Tangerine Peel

INGREDIENTS

2 baby pigeons
½ dried tangerine peel (soaked)
2 slices ginger
1 sprig spring onion (in sticks)
½ cup Shaoxing wine

SEASONINGS

1 tbsp soy sauce
¼ tsp salt
1 tsp sugar
1 tbsp oyster sauce
¼ cup water

PROCEDURES

1 Remove internal organs of pigeons, wash and then blanch in hot water.

2 Smear dark soy sauce on pigeons, blanch in oil and then set aside.

3 Heat up 2 tbsp of oil, put in ginger, spring onion and dried tangerine peel, and stir-fry. Add in fried pigeons and stir-fry.

4 Add in seasoning and Shaoxing wine, stew on high heat for about 5 minutes, turn it over, and then stew for another 5 minutes until cooked. Ready to serve.

材 料

乳鴿2隻
陳皮（浸透）½個
薑2片
葱（切段）1條
紹酒½杯

調味
醬油1湯匙
鹽¼茶匙
糖1茶匙
蠔油1湯匙
水¼杯

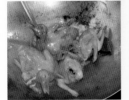

做 法

1 乳鴿去內臟，洗淨後飛水。

2 用老抽塗勻全身，走油備用。

3 燒熱油2湯匙，爆香薑葱及陳皮，放入已走油之乳鴿兜勻。

4 將調味及紹酒加入，用大火燜約5分鐘翻轉，再燜5分鐘至乳鴿熟透即成。

芝士焗蟹缽

Baked Crab Meat Bowl with Cheese

時間：20分鐘
份量：可做14杯（每杯約80克）
Processing time: 20 minute
Serving: 14 cups (80g each

材料

方包3片
蟹肉6兩（240克）
洋葱1個（切細粒）
大蘑菇1罐（切細粒）
煙肉6片（切細粒）

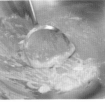

麵撈
牛油3安士
麵粉70克
清水275克
鮮奶80克

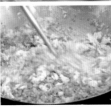

調味
雞粉2茶匙
芝士粉½湯匙

灑面用
麵包糠適量
芝士粉適量

做 法

1 洋葱、蘑菇、煙肉，以少許油炒
  香，加入1茶匙雞粉炒透，盛起。

2 牛油炒麵粉加水、奶，炒成麵撈。
  加入調味拌勻備用。

3 傾下蟹肉拌勻成餡料。

4 釀入容器中，灑上麵包糠，放上麵
  包，置焗爐以火力180℃焗至金黃
  即成。

INGREDIENTS

3 slices bread
240g crab meat
1 onion (finely diced)
1 can mushrooms (finely diced)
6 slices smoked bacon (finely diced)

STIR-FRIED BATTER
3 ounces butter
70g flour
275g water
80g milk

SEASONINGS
2 tsp chicken powder
½ tbsp cheese powder

SPRINKLE ON TOP
Some bread crumbs
Some cheese powder

PROCEDURES

1 Stir-fry onion, mushroom and bacon
  with a little oil. Add in 1 tsp chicken
  powder, stir-fry and take it out.

2 Stir-fry butter with flour, add in water
  and milk to fry into a batter. Add in
  seasonings and set aside.

3 Put in crab meat and mix into filling.

4 Stuff the filling into a container,
  sprinkle some bread crumbs on top,
  cover with a slice of bread, and bake in
  an oven at 180℃ until golden brown.
  Ready to serve.

五柳貴妃龍脷卷

Sweet and Sour Sole Fillet Rolls

時間：15分鐘
份量：4-6人
Processing time: 15 minute
Serving: 4-6 person

材　料

龍脷柳400克

火腿40克

肉葱120克

五柳料80克

糖醋140克

乾生粉（撲粉）適量

芡汁

糖1湯匙

雞粉1茶匙

水1/2杯

生粉2茶匙

雞醬2湯匙

醃料

鹽1/2茶匙

味粉1/4茶匙

胡椒粉少許

麻油少許

做　法

1　魚肉切成14片薄片，加入醃料醃片刻。

2　將魚片鋪平，放上火腿及葱段在魚肉上捲成魚卷。

3　上乾生粉，用中火油炸至金黃色盛起。

4　用1湯匙油起鑊，倒下五柳醬及芡料煮滾，淋在魚卷上即成。

INGREDIENTS

400g sole fillet

40g ham

120g skinned spring onion

80g pickled sweet and sour vegetables

140g sweet vinegar

Some cornstarch (for coating)

THICKENING SAUCE INGREDIENTS

1 tbsp sugar

1 tsp chicken powder

½ cup water

2 tsp cornstarch

2 tbsp chicken sauce

MARINADES

½ tsp salt

¼ tsp MSG

A little pepper

A little sesame oil

PROCEDURES

1　Cut fish fillet into 14 thin slices, add in the marinades to marinate for a while.

2　Place fish flat on a table, put ham and spring onion on it, and then roll it up.

3　Coat with cornstarch, deep-fry in oil on medium heat until golden brown, and take it out.

4　Put a tbsp of oil in a wok, pour in pickled sweet and sour vegetables, and thickening sauce, and bring it to a boil. Pour it over fish rolls and serve.

香芒咖喱乾炒蝦球

Curry Prawns with Mangoes

時間：15分鐘
份量：4-6人
Processing time: 15 minute
Serving: 4-6 person

INGREDIENTS

2 mangoes
600g prawns
Some basil
3 red chilies (finely diced)
1 tbsp curry paste
1 tsp minced garlic
1 tsp butter

材料

芒果2個

大蝦1斤（約600克）

九層塔適量

紅辣椒仔（切粒）3隻

咖喱醬1湯匙

蒜蓉1茶匙

牛油1茶匙

SEASONINGS

¼ tsp salt
1 tsp sugar
1 tsp chicken powder
Some pepper

MARINADES FOR PRAWNS

1 tbsp egg white
¼ tsp salt
1 tsp cornstarch

調味

鹽¼茶匙

糖1茶匙

雞粉1茶匙

胡椒粉少許

PROCEDURES

1   Shell prawns, wash and cut open their backs. Add in marinades and mix well. Blanch in hot oil and set aside.

2   Peel mangoes, cut into pieces and set aside.

3   Deep-fry basil leaves in hot oil to crispy and then take them out.

4   Heat up a wok, add in butter, put in red chilies, curry sauces, minced garlic and seasonings and then stir-fry.

5   Put prawns and mangoes into the pan, stir-fry quickly, and then serve it on a dish.

醃蝦

蛋白1湯匙

鹽¼茶匙

生粉1茶匙

做 法

1   蝦去殼，洗淨起雙飛，加入醃料拌匀，泡滾油備用。

2   芒果去皮，切塊備用。

3   九層塔摘葉，放熱油中炸脆盛起。

4   鑊燒熱後下牛油，加入紅辣椒粒、咖喱醬、蒜蓉及調味，一同炒香。

5   將蝦及芒果回鑊，快手炒匀，即可上碟。

魚羊燒鮮

Fried Mutton in Fish

時間：20分鐘
份量：4-6人
Processing time: 20 minute.
Serving: 4-6 person.

材 料

羊肉（攪爛）4兩（150克）
桂花魚10兩（400克）
葱絲適量

醬汁

茄汁3湯匙
鎮江香醋1湯匙
黃糖2湯匙
喼汁1茶匙
生粉2茶匙
清水1/2杯

醃料

13香料粉1/2茶匙
孜然粉1/4茶匙
蠔油1茶匙
醬油1茶匙
腐乳1/2磚
蛋黃1隻
糖1/4茶匙
生粉1湯匙
熟油1茶匙
麻油少許

蛋麵糊

蛋黃2隻
生粉1湯匙

做 法

1　羊肉加入醃料攪勻。

2　桂花魚去骨，用蛋麵糊塗勻，將羊
　　肉釀入魚中。

3　鑊中注入多量油，燒至八成熱，放
　　下桂魚，以慢火浸約4分鐘。

4　將魚盛起，轉放平底鍋中，以滾油
　　煎香釀有羊肉的一面。

5　醬汁煮滾淋在魚面，放上葱絲即成。

INGREDIENTS

150g mutton (minced)
400g grouper
Some shredded spring onion

SAUCE INGREDIENTS

3 tbsp tomato sauce
1 tbsp dark vinegar
2 tbsp brow sugar
1 tsp Worcestershire Sauce
2 tsp cornstarch
½ cup water

MARINADES

½ tsp 13-spice powder
¼ tsp caraway powder
1 tsp oyster sauce
1 tsp soy sauce
½ cube fermented bean curd
1 egg yolk
¼ tsp sugar
1 tbsp cornstarch
1 tsp cooked oil
A little sesame oil

EGG BATTER

2 egg yolks
1 tbsp cornstarch

PROCEDURES

1　Add marinades into mutton and mix
　　well.

2　Debone grouper, smear with egg batter,
　　and then stuff mutton into the fish.

3　Heat up a large amount of oil in a
　　wok until medium hot. Add in fish and
　　deep-fry in oil on low heat for about 4
　　minutes.

4　Take out the fish, transfer it to a pan,
　　and pan-fry the side stuffed with
　　mutton with hot oil.

5　Boil the sauce and then pour it over
　　the fish. Sprinkle spring onion on top.
　　Ready to serve.

香蕉火腩蒜子燜大鱔

Stewed Eel with Roasted Pork and Bananas

材料

白鱔400克
燒腩仔160克
蒜肉60克
香蕉(切厚塊)240克
濕花菇80克
薑肉10克
葱(切度)2條

芡料
生粉1茶匙
清水4湯匙

醃料
鹽1/4茶匙
糖1/4茶匙
生粉1/2茶匙
醬油1/2茶匙
薑汁酒1茶匙

調味
醬油2湯匙
蠔油2湯匙
雞粉1茶匙
麻油1/2茶匙
胡椒粉少許
清水1/2杯

做 法

1　白鱔洗淨瀝乾，加醃料拌勻。

2　放滾油中炸至金黃色盛起。

3　餘油將蒜子略炸備用。

4　燒熱瓦煲，落油，爆香薑、蒜子，加入冬菇及燒腩，灒酒下調味煮沸。

5　傾下白鱔以大火焗10分鐘至汁液剩餘1/4杯時，加入香蕉及葱度，再焗3分鐘，打芡上碟。

INGREDIENTS

400g eel
160g roasted pork
60g garlic
240g banana (in thick slices)
80g soaked mushrooms
10g ginger
2 sprigs spring onion (strip)

THICKENING SAUCE INGREDIENTS

1 tsp cornstarch
4 tbsp water

MARINADES

¼ tsp salt
¼ tsp sugar
½ tsp cornstarch
½ tsp soy sauce
1 tsp ginger juice

SEASONINGS

2 tbsp soy sauce
2 tbsp oyster sauce
1 tsp chicken powder
½ tsp sesame oil
A little pepper
½ cup water

PROCEDURES

1　Wash eel and then strain. Add in marinades and mix well.

2　Deep-fry it in hot oil until golden brown. Take it out and set aside.

3　Deep-fry garlic in the remaining oil and then set aside.

4　Heat up a clay pot, add in some oil, put in ginger, garlic, mushrooms and roasted pork, and then splash in some wine. Bring it to a boil.

5　Put in eel and stew on high heat for 10 minutes until sauce is reduced to ¼ cup. Add in bananas and spring onion, and stew for another 3 minutes. Stir in thickening sauce and then dish.

麻辣雞丁

Spicy Stir-fried Chicken

時間：25分鐘
份量：6-8人
Processing time: 25 minutes
Serving: 6-8 persons

材料

麻辣花生1½兩（60克）

蒜心或四季豆（切粒）2兩（80克）

雞腿肉8兩（300克）

辣椒乾½兩（10克）

蒜蓉2茶匙

薑蓉1茶匙

生粉適量

醃雞料

蛋黃½隻

醬油2茶匙

蠔油1茶匙

生粉½湯匙

熟油1湯匙

調味

醬油½湯匙

鎮江香醋½茶匙

黃砂糖½茶匙

生粉½茶匙

水2湯匙

做法

1　雞切丁塊，用醃料拌勻，炸前再撲乾生粉。

2　燒油八成熱，放下雞肉炸至金黃，略乾身盛起。

3　燒油少許，放下辣椒、蒜蓉、薑蓉爆香，傾下雞肉、麻辣花生和蒜心。

4　加調味拌勻上碟。

註：如果用四季豆必須飛水、過冷；蒜心就不用飛水。

INGREDIENTS

60g hot and spicy peanuts

80g garlic shoots or French beans (diced)

300g chicken thigh meat

10g dried chili

2 tbsp minced garlic

1 tsp minced ginger

Some cornstarch

CHICKEN MARINADES

½ egg

2 tsp soy sauce

1 tsp oyster sauce

½ tbsp cornstarch

1 tbsp cooked oil

SEASONINGS

½ tbsp soy sauce

½ tsp dark vinegar

½ tsp brown sugar

½ tsp cornstarch

2 tbsp water

PROCEDURES

1　Cut chicken meat into cubes, mix with marinades, coat with cornstarch before deep-frying.

2　Heat some oil until medium hot. Deep-fry chicken it in until golden brown and then take it out.

3　Heat up a little oil, add in chili, minced garlic and minced ginger, and stir-fry. Then put in chicken, spicy peanuts and beans.

4　Add in seasonings, stir-fry and then dish.

NOTE: French beans have to be blanched in hot water and then rinsed with tap water but not for garlic shoots.

黃金炒木須肉

Stir-fried Pork with Eggs

時間：15分鐘
份量：4-6人
Processing time: 15 minutes
Serving: 4-6 persons

材料

新鮮半肥肉160克
濕木耳40克
雞蛋160克
肉葱40克
蒜肉10克

醃肉料

醬油1茶匙
熟油1茶匙
糖1/4茶匙
生粉1/2茶匙
水1/2茶匙

調味料

豆瓣醬1茶匙
海鮮醬1茶匙
醬油2茶匙
雞粉1/2茶匙
胡椒粉少許
麻油少許

做法

1 豬肉切粗絲，用醃料拌匀，泡油備用。

2 雞蛋打散，木耳切絲。

3 蒜蓉起鑊，爆熟肉絲及木耳，加入調味兜匀，盛起。

4 鑊加油燒熱，將雞蛋液傾下炒至半熟，將盛起之材料傾下，快手炒匀，灑下葱粒即成。

INGREDIENTS

160g pork with some fat
40g soaked wooden fungus
160g egg
40g skinned spring onion
10g minced garlic

MARINADES

1 tsp soy sauce
1 tsp cooked oil
¼ tsp sugar
½ tsp cornstarch
½ tsp water

SEASONINGS

1 tsp broad bean sauce
1 tsp hoisin sauce
2 tsp soy sauce
½ tsp chicken powder
A little pepper
A little sesame oil

PROCEDURES

1 Cut pork into strips, mix with marinades, blanch in oil and set aside.

2 Beat the eggs and cut wooden fungus into shreds.

3 Put minced garlic in a wok, add in cooked pork and wooden fungus, add in seasonings and stir-fry. Take it out and set aside.

4 Heat up some more oil in the wok, pour in egg liquid and stir-fry until half-cooked. Put in the ingredients from step (3) and stir-fry quickly. Sprinkle some spring onion dices and serve.

霸王豬肚

時間：3.5小時
份量：8-10人
Processing time: 3.5 hours
Serving: 8-10 persons

Braised Pig Abdomen with Glutinous Rice

材料

豬肚1個
糯米3兩（120克）
洋薏米1兩（40克）
白蓮子1兩（40克）
栗子肉2兩（80克）
白果2兩（80克）
冬菇4隻
瑤柱2粒
蝦米1兩（40克）
金華火腿1兩（40克）
薑米2湯匙
鹹蛋黃（壓蓉）2個（後下）
蟹黃2湯匙（後下）

調味

蠔油1湯匙
醬油2茶匙
鹽1/2茶匙
雞粉1茶匙
麻油少許
胡椒粉少許

芡料

上湯1/2杯
雞粉1/2茶匙
生粉1½茶匙
薑汁酒1茶匙

做法

1 豬肚去油，翻轉面，刮去潺液，再以生粉、鹽、油等洗擦多次，沖洗乾淨。

2 把豬肚飛水、過冷、瀝乾。

3 將糯米、薏米、蓮子、栗子、白果，分別浸透瀝乾。

4 冬菇浸透切粒；蝦米、瑤柱浸透撕開；火腿切粒。

5 燒油2湯匙爆香薑米，傾下以上各材料炒透，加入調味拌勻，釀入豬肚內。

6 豬肚隔水燉3小時至腍軟，用剪刀將豬肚剪成塊狀，再蓋上糯米料，伴以灼熟時菜。

7 芡料拌勻煮沸，加入鹹蛋黃蓉及蟹黃推勻，淋在豬肚面即成。

INGREDIENTS

1 pig abdomen
120g glutinous rice
40g raw job's tears
40g white lotus seeds
80g chestnuts (shelled)
80g gingko
4 shitake mushrooms
2 dried scallops
40g dried shrimps
40g dry Chinese ham
2 tbsp ginger (finely diced)
2 salted egg yolks (mashed, to be used later)
2 tbsp crab roe (to be used later)

SEASONINGS

1 tbsp oyster sauce
2 tsp soy sauce
½ tsp salt
1 tsp chicken powder
Some sesame oil
Some pepper

THICKENING SAUCES

½ cup broth
½ tsp chicken powder
1½ tsp cornstarch
1 tsp wine ginger juice

PROCEDURES

1 Remove fat of pig abdomen, turn it over and then scrape lime off its skin. Rub it with cornstarch, salt and oil several times and then wash thoroughly.

2 Blanch it in hot water, rinse with tap water, and then strain.

3 Soak glutinous rice, raw job's tears, lotus seeds, chestnuts and gingko separatey and then strain.

4 Cut mushrooms into dices. Soak dried shrimps and scallops until softened, and then shred. Cut dried ham into fine dices.

5 Heat up 2 tbsp of oil in a wok, stir-fry ginger dices, add in other ingredients and stir-fry thoroughly, and then stir in seasonings. Stuff the mixture into pig abdomen.

6 Double-boil pig abdomen above water for 3 hours until tender. Cut it into pieces with a pair of scissors. Place glutinous rice on top and decorate with some vegetables.

7 Mix thickening ingredients and bring it to a boil, add in salted egg yolk and crab roe, and stir well. Pour the sauce over pig abdomen. Ready to serve.

薇態梅姿

Double-boiled Rosy Shape Pork with Preserved Cabbage

材料

五花腩肉1½斤（900克）
梅菜4兩（160克）
薑2片
葱1條
紅辣椒仔2隻
木耳½兩（20克）

香料

白芷1片
桂皮1片
草果½個
茴香½茶匙
甘草1片
陳皮1角
丁香½茶匙

調味

醬油½杯
砂糖70克
麻油1茶匙

做 法

1 腩肉原件飛水；梅菜洗淨浸透切碎；
   木耳浸透備用。

2 白鑊爆梅菜至乾身，加入少許糖及
   1湯匙油兜勻，盛起備用。

3 燒紅鑊下油2湯匙，爆香薑、葱、
   辣椒及香料，灒酒下腩肉，注入過
   面清水及調味以中火燜30分鐘。

4 將肉取起待凍，切成丁方12塊。

5 每塊肉再片成長形，加進適量梅
   菜，成玫瑰花狀。

6 做12朵扣在碗中，以木耳圍邊，注
   入原汁，以大火燉3小時。

7 取出潷出汁液，反扣深碟，以已灼時
   菜伴邊，原汁煮沸，淋回肉中即成。

INGREDIENTS

900g pork belly
160g preserved cabbage
2 slices ginger
1 sprig spring onion
2 red chilies
20g wooden fungus

SPICES

1 slice Dahurian Angelica
1 slice cinnamon
½ tsaoko
½ tsp fennel
1 slice licorice root
1 pc dried tangerine peel
½ tsp clove

SEASONINGS

½ cup soy sauce
70g sugar
1 tsp sesame oil

PROCEDURES

1 Blanch whole piece of pork belly in hot
   water. Wash preserved cabbage, soak
   and then chop finely. Soak wooden
   fungus and set aside.

2 Stir-fry preserved cabbage in a dry
   wok until dried. Add in a little sugar
   and 1 tbsp of oil and stir-fry. Take it
   out and set aside.

3 Heat up wok, add in 2 tbsp of oil, put
   in ginger, spring onion, chili and spices,
   pour in wine and then put in pork belly.
   Fill in water until it is slightly above
   the ingredients. Add in seasonings
   and simmer it on medium heat for 30
   minutes.

4 Take out the pork, leave it to cool, and
   then cut into 12 cubes.

5 Cut each cube into rectangular pieces,
   add in some preserved cabbage and
   shape into a rose.

6 Put 12 pork roses in a bowl, surround
   it with preserved cabbage, and then
   pour in the sauce from previous
   simmering. Double boil it above water
   for 3 hours.

7 Take out the sauce, flip the bowl over
   to transfer the pork onto a plate
   and then decorate with blanched
   vegetables. Heat up the pork sauce
   from cooking and then pour it over
   the meat. Ready to serve.

竹葉青蔥香燒肉

Stewed Pork with Wine

材料

五花腩肉（切塊）1斤（600克）

肉葱3兩（120克）

薑片1兩（40克）

醬油½杯

冰糖1粒

老抽少許

清水適量

竹葉青酒120克

做法

1 五花腩肉洗淨飛水，過冷後以老抽上色。

2 燒滾油，傾下豬肉，炸至金黃盛起瀝乾。

3 燒油爆薑、葱，加入已炸好之肉塊放下兜匀。

4 潛入竹葉青，加入冰糖及過面清水、醬油等，煮滾後約10分鐘，轉落瓦煲中。

5 改中慢火燜至肉腍(約1小時)便可上碟。

INGREDIENTS

600g pork belly (cut into pieces)

120g skinned spring onion

40g ginger slices

½ cup soy sauce

1 pc rock sugar

some dark soy sauce

Some water

120g Chinese white wine (Zhuye Qing Jiu)

PROCEDURES

1 Wash pork belly, blanch in hot water, rinse with tap water and then mix with dark soy sauce.

2 Heat up some oil, put in pork, deep-fry until golden brown, take it out and strain off excess oil.

3 Heat up some oil, add in ginger and spring onion, add in the deep-fried pork and stir-fry.

4 Splash in white wine, add in rock sugar and fill in water until it is slightly above ingredients. Bring it to a boil and cook for another 10 minutes. Transfer the pork to a clay pot.

5 Stew on low to medium heat for about an hour until the meat is tender. Place it on a dish and serve.

啤酒柱侯燜牛尾

Stewed Ox Tail with Beer

材料

牛尾800克
甘筍320克
洋葱120克
蒜肉60克
青島啤酒1罐

醬料
柱侯醬2½湯匙
海鮮醬2湯匙

調味
冰糖¾兩（27克）
醬油3湯匙
雞粉1茶匙
鹽½茶匙

香料
香葉4片
草果1個
八角3粒

做法

1 牛尾切段、飛水、瀝乾。

2 洋葱用少許油略炒香，盛起。

3 燒油爆香蒜肉及香料，加入醬料和
  牛尾炒透，注入過面清水，煮滾後
  以中慢火燜約1½小時。

4 將甘筍和啤酒加入再燜½小時，傾
  下已炒之洋葱兜勻上碟。

INGREDIENTS
800g ox tail
320g carrot
120g onion
60g garlic
1 can beer (Qingdao Beer)

SAUCE INGREDIENTS
2½ tbsp chuhou Paste
2 tbsp Hoisin Sauce

SEASONINGS
27g rock sugar
3 tbsp soy sauce
1 tsp chicken powder
½ tsp salt

HERBS
4 bay leaves
1 tsaoko
3 star aniseeds

PROCEDURES

1 Cut ox tail into pieces, blanch in hot
  water and then strain.

2 Stir-fry onion with a little oil and then
  take it out.

3 Stir-fry garlic and herbs with a little
  oil, add in sauce ingredients and ox
  tail, and stir-fry. Fill in water until it
  is slightly above ingredients, bring it
  to a boil and then simmer on medium
  to low heat for 1½ hours.

4 Add in carrots and beer, and stew for
  another half an hour. Put in stir-fried
  onion and stir-fry. Ready to serve.

醬燒紐西蘭羊鞍扒

Roasted Lamb Chop with Special Sauce

材料

紐西蘭羊鞍扒500克

蒜肉15克

黑椒碎5克

醃料

蠔油1/2杯

海鮮醬3湯匙

醬油1/4杯

威士忌3湯匙

蒜蓉1茶匙

辣椒蓉1茶匙

糖1茶匙

水1/2杯

做法

1 將醃料開勻。

2 塗於整塊羊肋扒上（中途翻轉3-4
次），置雪櫃醃1/2天備用。

3 預熱焗爐250℃，將已醃好之羊扒
取出，放入焗爐焗約30分鐘至色澤
金黃。

4 取出羊扒，切件，上碟。

5 將醃肉汁料，加入黑椒碎煮滾，吃
時淋在羊扒上。

INGREDIENTS

500g New Zealand lamb chop
15g minced garlic
5g ground black pepper

MARINADES

½ cup oyster sauce
3 tbsp hoisin sauce
¼ cup soy sauce
3 tbsp whisky
1 tsp minced garlic
1 tsp minced chili
1 tsp sugar
½ cup water

PROCEDURES

1 Mix Marinades.

2 Smear it on lamb chop, turn it over
and repeat 3 to 4 times. Put it in a
refrigerator to marinade for ½ day.
Set aside.

3 Bake the lamb chop in a preheated
oven at 250℃ for 30 minutes until
golden brown.

4 Take it out, cut into pieces and then
dish.

5 Add black pepper to marinade sauce
and bring it to a boil. Pour it over the
lamb chop to serve.

南瓜汁鮮菌翡翠苗

Assorted Mushrooms and Pea Shoots in Pumpkin Sauce

INGREDIENTS

150g pumpkin
120g hsui tseng mushroom
1 cup lingzhi mushroom
400g pea shoots
1 garlic (sliced)

SEASONING

½ tsp salt

THICKENING SAUCE INGREDIENTS

1 tsp soy sauce
1 tsp chicken powder
1 cup broth
1 tsp cornstarch

PROCEDURES

1 Peel pumpkin, steam to cooked and then mash into purée. Set aside.
2 Wash mushrooms, blanch in hot water and then strain.
3 Heat up 2 tbsp of oil, stir-fry garlic in it, add in mushrooms and pea shoots, add in salt, stir-fry thoroughly, strain off excess water and then put it on a plate.
4 Mix pumpkin purée with thickening sauce ingredients and bring it to a boil. Pour the sauce over assorted mushrooms. Ready to serve.

材 料

南瓜150克
秀珍菇120克
靈芝菇1杯
翡翠豆苗400克
蒜頭(切片)1粒

調味
鹽1/2茶匙

芡料
醬油1茶匙
雞粉1茶匙
上湯1杯
生粉1茶匙

做 法

1 南瓜去皮、蒸熟、壓蓉備用。
2 雜菌洗淨、飛水、瀝乾。
3 燒油2湯匙爆香蒜片,傾下雜菌和翡翠苗,加鹽炒透盛起,瀝汁水後置碟中。
4 南瓜蓉加入芡料中拌勻煮滾,淋在雜菌面即成。

時間：10分鐘
份量：4-6人
Processing time: 10 minutes
Serving: 4-6 persons

上湯竹笙釀蘆筍

Bamboo Fungus and Asparagus in Broth

INGREDIENTS

40g dried bamboo fungus
360g Thai asparagus
1 tbsp matrimony vine
1 cup water
1 slice ginger

SEASONING

2 tsp dried scallop essence

PROCEDURES

1 Soak bamboo fungus, blanch in hot water, rinse, and then pat dry. Cut into rings of 1-inch long.

2 Blanch asparagus in hot water, rinse with tap water, and then strain. Put a bamboo fungus ring on it.

3 Put water into a pot, add in ginger and seasoning, and bring it to a boil. Add in asparagus and matrimony vine, cook for a short while and then serve.

材 料

乾竹笙40克
泰國蘆筍360克
杞子1湯匙
清水1杯
薑1片

調味
乾貝素2茶匙

做 法

1 竹笙浸透、飛水、過冷、壓乾水份，切成約1吋長的圓圈。

2 將蘆筍飛水、過冷、瀝乾，套入竹笙圈中。

3 清水置煲中，下薑片及調味煮滾，放下蘆筍和杞子，煮片刻即成。

平湖嫣翠

Steamed Egg with Crab Meat

INGREDIENTS

313g bitten melon juice (blend 1 bitter melon with ½ cup of broth)
3 eggs
Some crab roe
Some crab meat
Some gold foils

SEASONING

1 tsp salt

PROCEDURES

1 Mix bitter melon and broth with an electric blender into a juice.
2 Heat up bitter melon juice, add in seasoning and stir well.
3 Beat eggs, pour bitter melon juice into egg liquid, and then scoop out bubbles.
4 Pour into a bowl and then steam it on medium or low heat for 10 minutes.
5 Put some crab meat, crab roe and gold foils on it. Ready to serve.

材 料

涼瓜汁313克（涼瓜1個+上湯½杯攪汁）
雞蛋3隻
蟹黃適量
蟹肉適量
金箔適量

調味
鹽1茶匙

做 法

1 涼瓜與上湯置攪拌機內攪爛成汁。
2 涼瓜汁煮熱，加入調味拌勻。
3 雞蛋打散，再將涼瓜汁撞入蛋液中，撇去泡沫。
4 注入盅內，以中慢火蒸10分鐘。
5 面放蟹肉、蟹黃及金箔即成。

岐山羊肉湯

Qi Shan Mutton Soup

時間：40分鐘
份量：4人
Processing time: 40 minutes
Serving: 4 persons

INGREDIENTS

240g mutton
8 red dates (cored)
1 tbsp matrimony vine
1 fresh ginseng
1 Beijing scallion
6 garlic
100g vermicelli
¼ cup Shaoxing wine
4 cups chicken broth

SEASONING

Some salt

PROCEDURES

1 Cut mutton into slices.

2 Put red dates, matrimony vine and ginseng into a pot, pour in broth, and then simmer on medium or low heat for about 30 minutes.

3 Cut leek into slices, soak cellophane noodle in water and deep-fry garlic in hot oil.

4 Put vermicelli and garlic into the pot of broth.

5 Put in Beijing scallion and mutton, and then wine and seasoning. Ready to serve.

材料

羊肉6兩(240克)

紅棗(去核)8個

杞子1湯匙

鮮人參1枝

大葱1枝

蒜頭6粒

粉絲100克

紹酒¼杯

雞湯4杯

調味

鹽適量

做法

1 羊肉切片。

2 紅棗 、杞子、人參放鍋中,注入上湯,以中慢火煮約30分鐘(使其出味)。

3 大葱切片;粉絲浸透;蒜頭炸香。

4 將粉絲、蒜頭加進上湯中。

5 再把大葱、羊肉放下,最後加入紹酒和調味即成。

乳花石湯丸

Marble Glutinous Rice Balls

時間：15分鐘
份量：6-8人
Processing time: 15 minutes
Serving: 6-8 persons

INGREDIENTS

160g glutinous rice flour
2 tbsp rice flour
Some water
A little red, yellow, green and blue
  colourings

FILLING

120g red bean paste

PROCEDURES

1 Knead filling ingredients into small balls.
2 Put glutinous rice flour and rice flour into a basin. Add in some water and knead into dough.
3 Divide it into 5 portions and then mix each of them with a different colouring.
4 Make a small bowl shape with dough, wrap in a ball of filling, close its opening and then knead into a ball.
5 Bring half pot of water to a boil and then put in glutinous rice balls. When the water is boiling, add in a cup of cold water and cook until it boils again. When the balls float on water, take them out and serve.

材 料

糯米粉160克
粘米粉2湯匙
水適量
紅、黃、綠、藍色素各少許

餡料

豆沙3兩(120克)

做 法

1 將餡料搓成小粒。
2 糯米粉、粘米粉置盆中,以適量清水搓成軟硬適中之粉糰。
3 分成5份,每份加入不同色素搓透。
4 將粉糰捏一深窩,放入1粒餡料,收口搓圓。
5 燒半鍋水,水滾投入糯米球,大滾再加1杯凍水,待再滾起,見浮者便可撈出食用。

上湯素魚翅餃

Artificial Shark Fin Dumplings in Broth

時間：15分鐘
份量：6-8人
Processing time: 15 minute
Serving: 6-8 person

材料

餛飩皮14-16片
攪豬肉160克
素魚翅40克
濕發木耳10克
濕發冬菇35克(3隻)
馬蹄肉40克
已灼紹菜 / 椰菜120克

調味
醬油1茶匙
蠔油1湯匙
糖½茶匙
雞粉½茶匙
蛋白30克(1隻)
生粉1湯匙
水1湯匙

做 法

1 將魚翅浸軟,用沸水煮片刻(約2-3分鐘),過冷、瀝乾備用。
2 椰菜及紹菜飛水、過冷,瀝乾後剁碎。
3 馬蹄剁碎;木耳及冬菇浸透切粒。
4 將以上各料放盤中,加入調味攪透,置雪櫃雪½天,以餃子皮包成餃子狀。
5 放大滾水中煮熟即成。

註：煮餛飩時,先燒沸水至大滾,放入餛飩待煮至浮起,再下1杯水,待再次滾起,餛飩才能完全熟透。記着全程不能蓋鍋蓋。

INGREDIENTS

14-16 pcs Shanghai wonton sheet
160g minced pork
40g artifical shark fins
10g soaked wooden fungus
3 (35g) soaked mushrooms
40g water chestnuts (peeled)
120g Chinese cabbage (blanched in hot water)

SEASONINGS

1 tsp soy sauce
1 tbsp oyster sauce
½ tsp sugar
½ tsp chicken powder
1 (30g) egg white
1 tbsp cornstarch
1 tbsp water

PROCEDURES

1 Soak shark fins until softened, cook in boiling water for about 2 to 3 minutes, rinse with tap water, strain off excess water, and set aside.
2 Blanch Chinese cabbage in hot water, rinse with tap water, strain and then chop into fine pieces.
3 Chop water chestnuts finely. Soak wooden fungus and mushrooms, and then cut into fine dices.
4 Put all the above ingredients into a mixing bowl, add in seasonings and mix well. Store in a refrigerator for half a day and then wrap into dumplings with Shanghai wonton sheet.
5 Cook them in boiling water until cooked. Ready to serve.

NOTE: Cook dumplings in boiling water. When they float on the water, add in 1 cup of water and bring it to a boil. When the dumplings float again, they are well cooked. Remember to leave the pot open in cooking.

魚翅菇瑤辦麵

Shark Fins and Mushrooms with Chinese Fettuccine

時間：15分鐘
份量：6-8人
Processing time: 15 minutes
Serving: 6-8 persons

INGREDIENTS

3 mushrooms
2 dried scallops
80g soaked shark fin
240g Chinese fettuccine
2 slices ginger (shredded)
Some spring onion (shredded)

SEASONINGS

1 cup chicken broth
2 tbsp oyster sauce
2 tsp soy sauce
Some sesame oil
Some pepper
2 tsp cornstarch

PROCEDURES

1 Soak mushrooms in water and then shred. Soak dried scallops and then tear them into shreds.
2 Put noodles into half pot of boiling water. When the water is boiling again and the fettuccine are loosened, take them out and strain.
3 Mix with a few drops of cooked oil and transfer it to a large plate. Set aside.
4 Heat up 2 tbsp of oil, stir in ginger, mushrooms and dried scallops, and then add in seasonings and soaked shark fins.
5 Leave it for a while and then pour it over the fettuccine. Ready to serve.

材料

冬菇3隻
瑤柱2粒
濕發魚翅2兩（80克）
寬條蛋麵6兩（240克）
薑（切絲）2片
葱絲適量

調味
雞湯1杯
蠔油2湯匙
醬油2茶匙
麻油少許
胡椒粉少許
生粉2茶匙

做法

1 冬菇浸透切絲；瑤柱浸透撕開。
2 燒水半鍋至沸滾，將麵放下，待其翻滾麵條鬆開，隨即盛起瀝乾。
3 滴入少許熟油拌勻，置大碟中備用。
4 燒油2湯匙，爆香薑絲、冬菇和瑤柱，加入調味及已發好之魚翅。
5 待滾片刻，即可淋在麵條上。

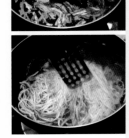

黃金蟹苗炒飯

Fried Rice with Crab Roe

時間：15分鐘
份量：6-8人
Processing time: 15 minutes
Serving: 6-8 persons

INGREDIENTS

80g crab roe
2 bowls rice
Some spring onion (finely diced)
2 tbsp ginger (finely diced)
1 egg (beaten)

SEASONINGS

½ tsp salt
½ tsp chicken powder
1 tbsp Shaoxing wine

PROCEDURES

1 Stir-fry ginger in hot oil.
2 Add in rice and egg, and stir-fry thoroughly.
3 Splash in some wine, add in seasoning and stir-fry.
4 Add in crab roe and spring onion, and stir-fry. Ready to serve.

材 料

蟛蜞膏2兩（80克）

白飯2碗

葱（切粒）適量

薑米2湯匙

雞蛋（打散）1隻

調味

鹽½茶匙

雞粉½茶匙

紹酒1湯匙

做 法

1 用油爆香薑米。

2 加入白飯和雞蛋炒至散開。

3 灒酒，下調味炒透。

4 最後加入蟛蜞膏及葱粒即成兜勻。

野葛菜水

Yellowcress Tea

INGREDIENTS

450g fresh yellowcress
5 honey dates
1 dried tangerine peel
40g apricot seed
3 litres water

PROCEDURES

1 Wash yellowcress with roots intact thoroughly.

2 Place kudzu vine, honey dates, dried tangerine peel and apricot seed into a pot.

3 Add in some water, bring it to a boil, and then lower the heat to medium or low and boil for another hour.

NOTE: This soup can relieve febrile sickness and body fatigue.

材 料

新鮮野葛菜12兩（450克）
蜜棗5個
陳皮1角
南北杏1兩（40克）
清水3公升

做 法

1 野葛菜原棵連根洗淨。

2 將葛菜、蜜棗、陳皮和南北杏放入煲中。

3 加入適量清水，滾後以中慢火煲1小時。

註：此湯可清燥及有消除筋骨痛之效。

肉桂紅棗茶

Cinnamon and Red Dates Tea

INGREDIENTS

2 slices (5g) cinnamon
12 red dates (cored, cut 3 of them into fine dices)
1 slice ginger
4 cups water
Some honey
Some pine seeds

PROCEDURES

1 Wash cinnamon, red dates and ginger and then put them in a pot. Add in water and cook for about 2 minutes. Then turn off the heat.

2 Filter out cinnamon, red dates and ginger.

3 Add in honey to the liquid and mix well.

4 Cover it with a lid for a short while and then ready to serve. It can also be served with pine seeds and red dates.

NOTE: It can be served cold.

材 料

肉桂2片（5克）
去核紅棗12個（3個切小粒）
薑1片
清水4杯
蜜糖適量
松子仁適量

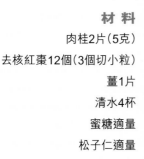

做 法

1 肉桂、紅棗、薑片洗淨置鍋中，注入清水煮約2分鐘，熄火。

2 潷清汁水，棄去肉桂、紅棗和薑片。

3 加入蜜糖拌勻。

4 加蓋焗片刻，便可進食。吃時加入松子仁和紅棗粒。

註：如要冷吃，可置雪櫃，凍食亦佳。

杞子桂花糕

Matrimony Vine and Sweet Osmanthus Pudding

時間：20分鐘
份量：4-6人
Processing Time: 20 minutes
Serving: 4-6 persons

INGREDIENTS

150g water chestnuts powder
240g rock sugar
2 tbsp sweet-scented osmanthus
2 tbsp matrimony vine
1 tsp oil
2¾ cups (687.5g) water

PROCEDURES

1 Mix water chestnut powder with 1 cup of water.

2 Mix the remaining 1¾ cups of water with rock sugar and sweet-scented osmanthus, and cook until sugar dissolves.

3 Add oil and matrimony vine, and turn off the heat when it is boiling.

4 Add in water chestnut mixture, and then stir quickly into a batter.

5 Pour it into a small mould and steam for 15 minutes. Ready to serve.

材 料

馬蹄粉4兩(150克)
冰糖6兩(240克)
桂花糖2湯匙
杞子2湯匙
油1茶匙
清水2¾杯(687.5克)

做 法

1 馬蹄粉先用1杯水開勻。

2 將餘下之1¾杯水加入冰糖及桂花糖同煮至糖溶。

3 加油及杞子,待滾熄火。

4 將調勻之馬蹄粉水加入,快手攪勻成稀糊狀。

5 倒落小模中,蒸15分鐘即成。

紅棗南瓜盅

Steamed Red Dates in a Pumpkin

時間：1小時
份量：6-8人
Processing time: 1 hour
Serving: 6-8 persons

1 small pumpkin
160g red dates (stoned)

PROCEDURES

1　Cut open pumpkin at top and remove its seeds. Wash and strain off excess water.

2　Remove stones of red dates, and then soak in water for about 30 minutes.

3　Put all red dates into the pumpkin, and then put it on a plate.

4　Steam it in a steamer on high heat for an hour and a delightful dessert is ready to serve.

材　料
小南瓜1個

紅棗（去核）160克

做　法

1　南瓜開蓋去籽，洗淨瀝乾水份。

2　紅棗去核，用水浸透約30分鐘。

3　將紅棗全放入南瓜盅內，用碟盛着。

4　置蒸籠以大火蒸1小時，即成一款清甜可口的甜品。

蜜汁心太軟

Glutinous Rice Balls in Honeyed Red Dates

時間：15分鐘
份量：4-6人
Processing time: 15 minutes
Serving: 4-6 persons

INGREDIENTS

40g glutinous rice flour
½ tbsp rice flour
40g water
20g large red dates (stoned)
2 tbsp honey

PROCEDURES

1　Remove stones of red dates, wash and then soak in water for 30 minutes.
2　Mix glutinous rice flour and rice flour with water and knead into dough. Set aside.
3　Stuff some dough into red dates, dish, and steam it in a steamer on high heat for 10 minutes. Take it out and leave to cool.
4　Deep-fry red dates in medium hot oil until golden brown. Take them out and mix with honey quickly. Ready to serve.

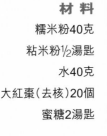

材 料

糯米粉40克
粘米粉½湯匙
水40克
大紅棗（去核）20個
蜜糖2湯匙

做 法

1　紅棗去核，洗淨，浸30分鐘。
2　糯米粉和粘米粉加水搓成糰備用。
3　將適量粉糰釀入紅棗中，用碟盛着，置蒸籠，以大火蒸10分鐘取出，待凍。
4　將紅棗放八成熱油中，傾下已炸之紅棗，快手拌入蜜糖，拌勻即成。

私房烹調秘笈
TIPS OF COOKING

甜酒釀
Sweet Rice Wine

- 上海南貨舖可以買到酒釀，約10-12元一盒。
- 酒釀可以做酒醋丸子、醋溜魚片等菜餚。
- 外省人愛用酒釀作菜，因它有特別的香氣。
- 通常酒醋汁液會在菜餚接近製作完成時才落，過早放入或加入調味料中，會使其酒香流失，菜餚便不能盡善盡美。
- 酒醋中的糯米特別香甜可口，可以作點心或加入糯米粉同搓，製成湯丸。有些人更把它當成零食小吃，不加製作便從盒中舀出往嘴裏送，風味頗為獨特。
- 在本書第11頁食譜的做法中説及：以清水沖淨（但不能用冷開水）的意思，是指不能用冰水，用自來清水沖便可以了。沖後待略乾便可用，無需太乾。
- 放入煲時亦要留意，不要壓得太實，以免酒汁難釀出。應該輕輕地放，放得略為鬆一點，這樣酒汁才容易滲出。
- 約三、四天便會有酒汁滲出，如仍沒有，可再蓋密。溫度是主要影響因素，所以只置放在溫暖地方便可，過高的溫度不宜。
- 酒汁出來後，用瓶裝好才可放雪櫃，酒汁未出，不宜放雪櫃。

- It can be bought at about HK$10-12 per box in Shanghainese produce stores.
- It can be made into delicious dishes like sweet soup with fermented glutinous rice balls and rice wine, and braised fish fillets with fermented glutinous rice.
- Shanghainese like to cook with rice wine for its special fragrance.
- Fermented glutinous rice juice is usually added at the final stage of cooking. If it is added too early or mixed with seasoning, its fragrance is lost and the dish becomes less tasty.
- The glutinous rice in the wine is very delicious which can be used to make dim-sum or knead with glutinous rice flour into glutinous balls. Some people even take it as a snack on its own.
- According to the recipe, it has to be rinsed with tap water instead of icy water, and then leave for a short while to dry slightly.
- When it is put into a pot, don't press it too hard or wine juice cannot be brewed. Remember to put it gently to allow wine to seep through.
- Wine is normally brewed after 3 or 4 days. If there is none, cover it tightly with a lid again and place it in a warm but not hot place for brewing.
- Store the bottle in a refrigerator only after wine has come out.

客家糯米酒
Hakka-styled Glutinous Rice Wine

- 與上海的酒釀做法相似。但仍要留意一些事項，糯米浸過夜後略洗，用水沖乾淨，但不能沖至全凍，米要有少許溫暖為合（因全凍便難釀出酒汁）。
- 酒餅平均分成8份研碎。酒餅可以在上海店舖買到，形狀有圓形、方形，其形狀有點像老人家用來洗頭的茶仔。
- 舊社會時代，有賣散裝燒酒的店舖，在那裏買到的酒餅總比現今買到的質量好，做出來的酒效果也較理想。
- 做酒時，把一份糯米、一份酒餅、一份暖水，分層次地重複放入，當然以用大口的瓦砵較為方便。但如家中沒有這些器皿，而用高身的玻璃瓶，那麼做時便比較困難。我們可用另一個辦法處理，先把糯米飯及酒餅拌勻才放入瓶，但仍是要分8份，逐份放入再加2湯匙暖水，重複至作完為止。但無論用甚麼器皿都必須清潔，不能有任何油膩，否則糯米容易變壞甚或發臭等。
- 糯米釀出酒後，約3個星期才好把酒釀隔出，隔去酒釀後的酒液，顏色會因時間放久了而漸漸變深成茶色。酒當然是存放時間久一點更好，但親手釀製至出現酒汁是很有成功感，我的烹飪學生們便高興得火速把酒用光。各位會選擇儲存多久才用，便要看你對酒的要求了。

- It is similar to the making of Shanghainese fermented glutinous rice wine. However, when rinsing the soaked glutinous rice, rinse it slightly until it is lukewarm or wine cannot be brewed when the rice is cold.
- Divide the Chinese yeast cake into 8 portions and then grind. Chinese yeast cakes can be bought in Shanghainese produce stores. They come in round or square shapes and are brown in colour.
- The cakes can also be bought in old Chinese wine stores, which offer yeast cakes of high quality.
- In making the wine, put a portion of glutinous rice, a portion of yeast cake and a portion of warm water one after another into an urn, and then repeat this process. You may mix glutinous rice with yeast cake before putting them into the container in 8 separate portions as in the original method. It is more convenient to use a pottery urn with a large opening. If you don't have one, a glass jar is also fine. No matter which type of containers you use, remember to use a clean and grease-free one or it will ruin the rice and its taste.
- When the wine is brewed, leave it for 3 weeks before filtering out the residual fermented glutinous rice. The wine will become brownish and mature over time.

檸檬酒
Lemon Wine

- 做檸檬酒的靈感來自我的太婆,她製檸檬酒是全用檸檬片的,也必定要去核。此處我改用2個切片,2個榨汁的做法,分別是榨汁做出來的酒較濁不夠清,但比較快有檸檬酒喝,適合現今人士的個性要求。
- 冰糖不用煮,放入酒中便會自然溶化。
- 飲用時加點七喜及冰塊,是為佐膳佳品。

- This wine is inspired by my great grandmother, who used lemon slices without any seeds. I have modified her recipe a bit by using 2 lemons in slices and 2 lemons for juice only. The squeezed lemon juice makes the wine cloudy but it can help speeding up the whole process.
- Rock sugar naturally dissolves in the wine.
- It can be served with 7-up (Sprite) and ice as a cold beverage.

菩提酒
Grape Wine

- 其竅門在食譜中的注意事項已說明。但鄭重再提醒大家的,是酒在100日裏發酵的過程中。當酒液還未釀出時,絕對不可移動酒瓶,因為經移動後,酒便會發出酸味。

- Don't move the bottle of wine during fermentation or the wine will become sour.

欖豉醬
Olive and Black Beans Sauce

- 欖豉醬用途廣泛，可蒸魚、燜雞、炒涼瓜排骨、清炒蔬菜等，惹味可口。做多一點存放，作菜便很方便。
- 材料必須打碎。油是天然防腐劑，對醬料有保護作用，油份不夠，物料易變壞。
- 材料最少炒5分鐘至香，先加入B料的130克糖炒約2分鐘（不要炒太久），才將其他B料放入，如此作法的醬料，顏色特別有光澤也特別香，如果糖與其他材料同下，就沒有此效果。煮至滾起推芡便可，待完全凍後才入瓶，器皿必須乾淨蓋好，放雪櫃，可以存放好一段時間。

- Its usage is quite versatile and can be used for steamed fish, stewed chicken, stir-fried bitten melon with spare-ribs and stir-fried vegetable. You may make more of it in one go and store the excessive sauce for later use.
- The ingredients have to be ground. As oil is a natural preservative, it has to be used in sufficient amount to prevent the sauce from rottening.
- Stir-fry the ingredients for at least 5 minutes until aromatic. Then add in 130g sugar from Ingredients B and stir-fry for 2 minutes (but not too long) before putting in the rest of Ingredients B. This can make the sauce luster and smell good. When it is boiling, stir in a thickening sauce. Leave it to cool and then transfer it to a clean container for storage. Cover its lid tightly and keep it in a refrigerator for future use.

自製南乳
Homemade Fermented Red Taro Curd

- 竅門也是在食譜中說過。但有兩點要切記，芋頭必須搓至極爛，不夠爛是做不到的。放在室溫發酵也得找個溫暖的角落，室溫不暖很難發至起霉。

- Remember to mash taro into purée and then place it in a warm place for fermentation.

自製臘腸
Homemade Chinese Sausages

- 最好用汾酒（以前雜貨店有售，現在可到國貨公司買）；如真的買不到，便用玫瑰露酒。
- 肉不要用攪拌器攪碎，必須用刀切的方法，口感才會好。
- 要留意曬至極度乾身才好收藏存放。

- Fenjiu wine can be bought in Chinese produce stores. If it is not available, replace it with rose wine.
- Cut the meat finely with a knife instead of food mixer for a better texture.
- Expose the sausages to direct sunlight until completely dried before storing them for later use.

家鄉風肉
Country Dry-cure Ham

- 如你懂得做煙肉和臘肉，做風肉便必定沒問題。同樣是半斤一條。
- 要注意肉必須吹至極乾身，如果不是北風天，家中又沒有冷氣。可以用保鮮紙包好風肉放雪櫃中，利用雪櫃的冷空氣抽乾肉的水份，但切記不要放入冰格內，因冰格只會保持其濕度，不會使其乾身。

- The processing of dry-cure ham is similar to that of smoked bacon and dry bacon. Each piece of ham also weighs about 320g.
- This ham must be dried thoroughly. If the weather is humid and there is no air-conditioner at home, you may wrap it with cling paper and then dehydrate it in a refrigerator. However, don't put it in a freezer as it will maintain the ham's moisture rather than drying it.

自製煙肉
Homemade Smoked Bacon

- 五花腩最好用五層肉。腩肉分為3個等級，腩肉的前腹及後腹都不夠好，以肋條肉帶骨的豬腩肉最佳。
- 新鮮的肉要切得整齊是比較困難，我們有一個可行的辦法，是去相熟的肉檔，一次過買3斤至5斤，或把整塊豬腩肉買下來，請檔主代為起骨，但不要把毛燒去（回家後才拔淨毛），起骨後存放在肉檔的雪櫃內，把肉雪硬，第二天才取。取肉時並請檔主用電刀切割成半斤一條，狀如臘肉般大小。如真的沒有相熟的肉檔，亦可買凍肉公司的豬腩肉，但當然以新鮮的為佳。
- 市面有現成的花椒和八角粉出售，如果不想自己動手研製，可以買這些現貨來用，份量同樣用2茶匙便可。
- 花椒八角和鹽炒香才可擦肉，擦肉後要醃2天，其間要把肉轉身。
- 2天後用暖水洗淨，再用清水浸15分鐘，由於醃了2天，鹹味十足，不用擔心會把味浸去。浸後掛在當風處吹。
- 最好在北風天才做，如在天氣熱時做便只好開冷氣來吹。
- 用手觸摸，感覺乾爽，才可以煙燻。燻成美麗的黃色，食用時切出適當份量，餘下用保鮮紙包好放雪櫃。

- Use pork belly around the rib area.
- Buy 2 to 3 kg of pork from a friendly butcher and ask him to remove the ribs for you but not the pig hair (which should be plucked by yourself), and then freeze the pork in his refrigerator overnight until it is frozen. On the following day, ask the butcher to cut the meat into pieces of about 320g each, like a Chinese bacon, with an electric knife. If you cannot find a good butcher, use a piece of frozen pork belly instead.
- Peppercorn and star aniseed powder are available in stores and 2 tsp of it is needed.
- Stir-fry peppercorn, star aniseed and salt before rubbing it onto the pork. Then marinate it for 2 days and turn it over in between.
- After 2 days, wash it with warm water, and then soak it in water for 15 minutes. As it has been marinated for 2 days, its savoury will not be washed out by water. Hang in an airy place to dry.
- Make it when the weather is fine and dry or you may need to dry it with an air-conditioner.
- Check with your hands to see if it is perfectly dry. Then it can be smoked into a golden brown bacon. Cut the amount of bacon you need, and wrap the remaining portion with cling paper and store it in a refrigerator for future use.

臘肉
Dry Blanched Pork

- 臘肉與風肉、煙肉的程序有點不同。風肉及煙肉是生醃的,而臘肉是經過飛水程序,因此臘肉表面是熟了少許,內裏仍是生肉,是呈現半生熟狀態。如此過程,再塗醬後,做出來的感覺既乾身而瘦肉的部份又會特別深色。
- 醃製肉類,每1條的重量,一般都是以½斤作標準。至於如何請選肉、擦肉及切割,我在第131頁"自製煙肉"中已教,在此不再談。
- 請緊記,把肉穿好掛當風處風乾時,不能過乾,太乾身是不能上色,只吹½天便可,½天的時間肉是不會吹得太乾的,放心好了。

- The making of dry bacon is slightly different from that of dry-cured ham and smoked bacon. For dry-cured ham and smoked bacon, the meat are simply marinated raw while blanched bacon has to be blanched in hot water in the processing. Therefore, dry bacon is cooked on the surface but still raw inside. After brushing it with sauce, the lean part will become specially dark when dried.
- Each piece of preserved meat normally weighs about 300g. For the selection, rubbing and cutting of meat, please refer to "Homemade Smoked Bacon" recipe (p.131) for details.
- Remember to dry the meat by hanging it in an airy place for about half a day. Don't make it too dry, otherwise it cannot be coloured properly.

醬油仁稔
Renmen Berry in Soy Sauce

- 用鹽揉捏仁稔時，必須帶上手套，否則手容易擦損。
- 仁稔搓揉後，會由青綠變成少許黃色，但揉5分鐘後仍沒變色，便不用理它，因揉5分鐘已足夠。
- 煮溶的糖，必須放涼至全凍，才可放入仁稔，否則便不可口。
- 仁稔入瓶前要拍裂，如覺拍會使仁稔汁液濺出，可以用刀剖開的方法。
- 排放瓶中，放入醬油料，雖說醃一星期可以食用，但最好醃上三個月才吃，會更可口。
- 醬油仁稔可用來蒸魚、燜雞、或煮仁稔醬等。

- When mixing berries with salt, you must protect your hands with a pair of gloves.
- After mixing it for 5 minutes, some berries may change from green to yellow.
- Leave the melted sugar to cool down before putting in the berries or they will become less tasty.
- Crack the berries before putting them into a bottle. You may smash or cut it with a knife.
- Line them in a bottle, fill in soy sauce ingredients, and then leave it for at least 1 week, or 3 months for a better taste.
- It can be used for making steamed fish, stewed chicken or renmen berry sauce.

糯米酒醋雞
Braised Chicken with Fermented Glutinous Rice

- 既然有親手釀製的酒，不妨用來多作些菜式。此菜甚為補身，很適合坐月子食用。
- 雞斬件醃後，記着要泡油。薑的份量要比較多。最重要的是用酒作主料煮食物，最好不要下鹽和用鹽醃，否則食味會帶酸不好吃。
- 此菜食味清甜，煮時不要下其他調味料，吃時蘸醬油便可。

- This dish is a nutritive supplement for mothers after giving birth.
- The marinated chicken must be blanched in hot oil and large amount of ginger can be used. As wine is a main ingredient for this dish, one must not add in salt or marinate ingredients with salt or the food will turn sour.
- Don't add any other seasoning in cooking. Simply serve it with a dipping sauce.

秘製鹹香骨
Tasty Spare-ribs

- 此菜好吃之處，在於口感極佳，外面極脆而內裏仍保持肉汁，並且鹹魚與豬肉的味道十分匹配，鹹魚蒸肉餅所以流行而歷久不衰便是此原因。
- 用鹹魚蓉醃骨的時間最少是1小時，但醃過夜更加入味。
- 炸前撲乾粉，炸時要炸透。至於炸的技巧，我曾多次說過。此處油燒至八成滾放入，炸約6分鐘。
- 緊記把物料撈起後才熄火，否則物料會吸回油份，口感便會太油膩。

- The special feature of this dish is that the juice of the meat is trapped beneath a crispy surface, giving it a distinctive texture. In addition, the flavour of salted fish complements pork perfectly and steamed minced pork with salted fish has been a favourite homemade dish of all times.
- Marinate ribs with minced salty fish for at least an hour or overnight for a better taste.
- Coat the ribs with flour before deep-frying until cooked. For the best result, one should deep-fry the food in medium hot oil for about 6 minutes.
- Remember to take out all the food before turning off the heat. Otherwise, the food will absorb the oil and becomes oily.

荷芹炒臘肉
Stir-fried Dry Bacon with Snow Peas and Chinese Celery

- 用自製臘肉做菜才不會浪費。此為懷舊家鄉菜色，年近歲晚，芽菇當造，可加入3-4個切片同炒。我家鄉的做法，是把芽菇用刀拍鬆來炒，長輩們說如此比較好吃。
- 如加入芽菇便要把它先泡油，因芽菇含澱粉質，如不走油，除了易黏鑊，也會不好吃。

- Arrow heads are in season in winter. They are usually cut into slices for stir-frying. Some people like to loosen it by tapping with a knife before cooking.
- As arrow heads are high in carbohydrates, they have to be blanched with hot oil to reduce their stickiness.

麵醬油渣仁棯蒸頭腩
Steamed Fish Head Belly with Brown Bean Paste

- 只要是大條的魚，便甚麼魚類都可以用。
- 一般人都認為油渣會太肥，但由於油份已於炸油的過程清除，餘下的為脆口的肉渣，既甘香而又鬆脆，這個方法最好用來煮或蒸一些腥味重的海鮮。
- 我用的仁棯醬是自製的，但如果你沒有做，便只好買現成的。很多醬園如九龍或八珍醬園都有，但未必是醬油做的，有些是糖醋製的，但都可以用。
- 仁棯可起出皮肉切成小塊，核也可以用，味道一樣可口，只是核不能吃罷了。

- Any kinds of big fish will do.
- Fatty pork crisp is less oily than people think as most of the fat has been extracted in the deep-frying process. It is crispy and delicious, and can be added in cooking or steaming to remove the fishy smell of seafood.
- Renmen berry sauce Is available in Kowloon Sauce Company and Pak Chun Sauce Company. It can be preserved in soy sauce or sweet vinegar and either will do.
- Peel renmen berries and then cut its flesh into tiny pieces. Its core can also be used in cooking but not edible.

脆貝豆豉蒜燜涼瓜
Braised Dried Scallops with Bitter Melon

- 瑤柱浸透，撕開後再炸至脆身。
- 此菜式，可以用自製的欖豉醬來做，用1湯匙便可。
- 涼瓜要脸便要飛水，飛水後涼瓜容易變黃，可以浸於凍水中，隔清水份才炒，便可以保青綠。

- Soak dried scallops in water until softened, tear into shreds and then deep-fry in hot oil until crispy.
- You may use 1 tbsp of homemade olive and black bean sauce to make this dish.
- Blanching bitter melon in hot water can make its flesh tender but yellowish. You may soak it in cold water and then strain off excess water before stir-frying in order to retain its bright green colour.

欖豉醬蒸金鼓
Steamed Scat with Olive and Black Bean Paste

- 用自己製的醬料多做幾款菜式，會很有成功滿足感。
- 金鼓的樣子有點像神仙魚，以前價錢便宜，產量多。現今的價格提升了不少。
- 選購金鼓，以½斤至10兩為佳，太大條並不可口。如宴客人多，可多蒸幾條。
- 金鼓的鱗較細，必須打掉乾淨。魚鰭上的刺容易刺到手，當被刺到時會很痛及痛很久，要特別小心。
- 現今出現了一些優質魚場，金鼓亦是其中一種優質魚。優質魚每條身上都有標籤，購買時要留意，當然價格也略貴。

- It is very satisfying to make dishes with one's own sauces.
- Scats were cheap in the old days but have become much more expensive now.
- Select the scats weigh around 300g each. Don't choose the large ones as they are less delicious.
- Their scales are small and have to be scraped thoroughly before cooking. Their fins are spiky and have to be handled with extra care.
- The scats raised in quality fish farms are labelled individually with higher quality, and naturally, at a higher price.

家鄉風肉百頁結
Country Dry-cure Ham with Shanghainese Bean Curd Knots

- 因為教了大家自製鹹肉，所以教大家以它製作菜餚。鹹肉百頁結是上海菜式，可説是個湯菜，是佐飯佳餚。
- 百頁結是可以在南貨舖買到現成已打好結的一種。如沒有，可買百頁回來自己打。
- 煮百頁結如不下梳打粉，口感太結實，不夠腍便難消化。
- 下梳打粉後飛水，水的份量不要多，剛過百頁結面約1/4茶匙便夠，不要飛水太久，時間不可超過2分鐘，因過久會爛。飛水後別忘記過冷。

- You can use the homemade dry cure ham introduced in this book to make this Shanghainese dish. As it is served in soup, it can be eaten with rice.
- Bean curd knots can be bought from Shanghainese produce stores. If knots are not tied, you can do it yourself.
- Soda powder must be added in the processing of bean curd knots to make them tender and easy to digest.
- Add soda powder to the knots before blanching them in hot water. Don't blanch for too long and not more than 2 minutes or they will turn mashy. Remember to rinse in cold water afterwards.

酒釀窩蛋
Egg in Glutinous Rice Wine

- 此甜品口感清，但因其有酒釀關係，所以有開胃作用。
- 蛋打入後，立即熄火，因蛋有重量，會沉在底部，而糖水是煮滾的，上窩時，蛋便會變成半生熟，十分好吃。

- The glutinous rice wine in this dish can stimulate one's appetite.
- Once the eggs are added to the soup, turn off the heat immediately. Due to the weight of eggs, they will sink to the bottom of hot soup and become half-cooked when served.

醋溜骨香魚
Braised Fish Fillet with Fermented Glutinous Rice

- 此魚我用了酒醋來製作，選用酸甜味配合。如要改別的味道也可以，例如用欖豉醬炒或加西芹、雜菌等炒製皆宜。
- 起骨時要小心，魚鰭刺到手會十分痛，可用毛巾擋隔才起骨。
- 刀鋒要利才不會容易傷到手。用刀手勢要平，片出魚肉。
- 魚頭上粉後要炸至金黃，以筷子觸碰，感覺脆身便可。
- 芡汁煮滾淋在魚肉上便可，切莫把魚回鑊炒，口感會粗糙不滑。

- This dish uses fermented glutinous rice to complement its sweet and sour flavour. You may change the ingredients to your own taste by using olive and black bean paste, or adding celery or assorted mushrooms.
- Beware of fish bones and fins. You'd better cover the fish with a towel when boning.
- Cutting knife has to be sharp and cut the fillet in horizontal movement.
- Coat the fish head with flour before deep-frying it to golden brown. Check it with chopsticks to see if it is crispy.
- Don't return the fillet to the wok and stir-fry with thickening sauce. Simply pour the sauce over the fried fillet to serve.

酒釀豬肚
Braised Pig Abdomen with Rice Wine

- 此菜有個好意頭的名堂"金銀珠寶藏滿袋"，合新年喜慶用之懷舊菜。
- 荔枝和龍眼最好用新鮮的。如季節不合時，便只好用罐頭，那當然是沒有鮮品的味美。

- As a pig abdomen can symbolize a purse stuffed with lots of valuables, it is a traditional auspicious dish for new year celebration.
- It is best to use fresh lychees and longans, which can be replaced with canned ones when not in season.

魚皮花生
Crispy Peanuts

- 魚皮花生製作過程甚為有趣，可以用作親子活動，會很受小朋友歡迎。
- 南乳要壓成極爛，不夠爛做好會不美觀。
- 花生有多少，清水便要用多少。慢火煮1小時後，放笪箕吹至極乾透，必定要完全乾身才可。
- 市售的魚皮花生是美麗的橙紅色，這是用了色素（橙紅粉）之故，顏色美麗但不健康，如不想食太多色素，只好用醬油做色。
- 麵粉加清水及醬色（即珠油），要顏色夠深，珠油便要加多一點。
- 用麵粉包花生時，要包得薄一點，厚身會變成太大粒。
- 花生做好，待凍後入瓶，但也應盡快吃完，不要存放太久，以免變味。

- It is an interesting process to make this dish with your children at home. I am sure you will all love it.
- Fermented red bean curd must be mashed into purée.
- Equal amounts of peanuts and water have to be used. Boil it on low heat for an hour, leave the peanuts on a sieve until completely dry.
- Orange colouring added to crispy peanuts on sale is unhealthy and it is recommended to use soy sauce instead.
- Mix flour, water and fine dark soy sauce for coating. If you want darker colour, add more soy sauce.
- Coat peanuts with a thin layer of flour or the peanuts will become too big after frying.
- When the peanuts are made, leave them to cool before storing them in a bottle. Remember that they have a short shelf life and should be consumed as soon as possible.

麻辣花生
Hot and Spicy Peanuts

- 注意煮9分鐘使汁水收乾後，必定要吹至極乾。
- 先把香料以油炸香，目的在於要油充滿麻辣的香味，才用來炸花生，使花生有麻辣味。
- 香料炸至出味後要先行撈出。待花生炸至金黃撈起放涼至全凍後，把炸過的香料放回花生中拌匀，再一起存放，花生便會有極佳的麻辣效果。

- Peanuts must be cooked for 9 minutes until moisture reduced, and then leave in an airy place until thoroughly dry.
- Deep-fry spices in hot oil to make the oil spicy before deep-frying peanuts in it to for a hot and spicy flavour.
- When the oil becomes spicy, remove the spices from it. Then deep-fry peanuts until golden brown, take them out, and then leave them to cool. Mix the deep-fried spices with peanuts and keep them in a container for an extra spicy taste.

醬燒鴨下巴
Roasted Duck Jaws

- 一般是作為餐前小吃，可預早燜好，放雪櫃冰格內保存，可以存放一段時間也不變壞。
- 食用時取出放焗爐焗便可，用錫箔紙包裹一部份才焗，除了美觀外，也給予客人清潔和方便。
- 至於燜的時間，不宜太久，1/2小時已足夠，過臉口感不佳。
- 如嗜辣者，可加多一點豆瓣醬或加2隻辣椒，便更惹味。

- It can be served as an appertizer. You may stew it at your convenience and store it in a refrigerator for later use.
- Before baking, wrap part of each jaw with aluminum foil to make it more attractive and handy to eat.
- Don't overdo this dish or its texture will be ruined. Half an hour is enough.
- For spicy-food lovers, add a bit more chili bean sauce or 2 chilies for an extra hot flavour.

桂花燒腸
Fragrant Roasted Sausages

- 此為幾十年前的燒臘店流行食品之一，以當時的物價，算是貴價燒臘。由於製作繁瑣，現今很多燒臘店都不再買，青年人便少吃到。
- 腸衣通常會用羊腸衣，浸½小時便會軟身，緊記洗淨、出水、浸透及瀝乾水才用。
- 所有材料必須刀切，不能用攪拌機攪，攪肉的口感欠佳。
- 肥肉只用糖醃，雖然説醃6小時，但是醃過夜也無妨，因醃的時間越久便越爽口，是為"冰肉"；如醃的時間不夠，是沒有此效果的。
- 如有罐腸器當然方便及容易做，但家庭製作，一般都不會有此工具。我們可以用一個闊口而粗身的漏斗取代便可。
- 灌滿後，記得在燒腸上刺些小孔。
- 要燒好的腸美觀，可以在水中加點橙紅粉色素調勻，才把腸放入飛水。
- 焗時必須翻面1次，否則顏色不均勻，脆度也不佳。

- It was one of the most popular and expensive food in roasted food stores decades ago. As it is quite complicated to make, it is no longer widely available nowadays.
- Goat intestines are used for the sausage skin. Soak them for half an hour until softened. Remember to wash it thoroughly, blanch in hot water, soak and then strain before use.
- All ingredients have to be cut with a knife rather than an electric food mixer for better texture.
- The fatty pork has to be marinated with sugar for at least 6 hours or overnight. The longer the marinating period, the more elastic the meat.
- If you don't have a sausage filling machine, stuff the meat into intestines with a funnel.
- When a sausage is filled, pierce some holes on its surface.
- To make sausages more good-looking, add some orange colouring in water before putting in the sausages for blanching.
- Turn the sausages once during baking to make them more completely crispy.

涼皮寶玉手撕雞
Shredded Chicken with Green Beans Starch Sheet

- 這是個非常好的涼菜頭盤。
- 粉皮有以綠豆或馬鈴薯製成的，體質寒的朋友，宜選用馬鈴薯製的一種。形狀有大塊如大餅狀的和粗條狀的，亦有乾和濕之分別。我們這裏選用的是粗條狀馬鈴薯製的乾品，可在國貨公司買到。馬鈴薯的口感較粉中帶爽，卻沒有綠豆製的寒涼，是上佳之選。
- 粉皮的包裝上所說的浸製時間不要理會，我教大家的方法，是在食前1小時才浸，然後浸½小時已足夠，撈出放入大滾水中煮5分鐘，再浸於冰水中過冷，口感便會滑而脆口。
- 要做得成功，時間控制是非常重要。粉皮要在食前15分鐘才隔清水份拌調味料。過早調味便會太腍，影響口感。

- It is a very delicious cold appertizer.
- Noodle Sheets can be made of mung beans or potatoes. For those who are weak and afraid of coldness, select the potato noodles. They come in large round sheets or broad sticks, dried or wet. I made this dish with dried potato noodle in broad sticks from a Chinese products store.
- Ignore the preparation suggestion printed on the box of noodles and follow mine: one hour before use, soak the noodles for half an hour, take them out and cook it in boiling water for 5 minutes. Then soak them in icy water for a short while to make them smooth and firm.
- Good timing is crucial to the success of this dish. Remember to strain off excess water of the noodles 15 minutes before serving, and then mix with seasoning to taste.

涼拌芥辣雞
Chicken and Cucumber with Mustard Oil

- 芥辣味獨特且刺激食慾，是個相當受歡迎的菜餚。
- 芥辣油含濃香的芥辣味，再加點青芥醬調勻，食味一流。芥辣油國貨公司有售。
- 用現成的瑞士汁浸雞，做法可口而簡單。浸雞料大滾後，把雞完全放入，要再提起，把雞肚內的水倒出，如是者重複做3次（為使雞肚先熟），然後才把雞整隻浸入鹵汁中（必須過面），浸20分鐘即可。有些朋友喜愛雞熟一點的，可以多浸5分鐘，但肉便會沒那麼嫩滑。
- 注意要凍後才斬件，味料調好食時淋上。

- Mustard oil has an unique flavour which can stimulate appetite.
- Mustard oil has a strong mustard taste and can be mixed with some mustard sauce for a great taste. It is available in Chinese products stores.
- It is delicious and easy to make by using ready-to-use swiss sauce. Bring the chicken blanching ingredients to a boil, submerge the whole chicken in it, take it out and pour out the liquid in the body, and repeat this process thrice until the chicken abdomen is well done. Then soak the whole chicken in stewing sauce completely for 20 minutes. For those who like to have it well done, soak the chicken for 5 more minutes but the meat may become less tender.
- Leave it to cool before chopping it up into pieces. Then pour the mixed seasoning over and serve.

五柳貴妃龍脷卷
Sweet and Sour Sole Fillet Rolls

- 只要是白色肉的魚，便甚麼魚柳也可用。
- 葱有粗細，我們要用大肉葱之葱白的一段。一般魚卷多用火腿、西芹、紅蘿蔔、冬菇和中芹等。今次只用火腿配肉葱，有特別的香氣。

- Any white meat fish will do.
- Use the white portion of skinned large spring onion for its unique aroma.

燒鴨
Roasted Duck

- 燒鴨雖然在燒臘店可以很容易買到，但這裏所說的是住家式的燒鴨製作，別具風味。
- 此鴨與燒臘店製作的分別是不用吹氣，並且只用鹽醃，也許你會覺得食味單調，但健康。如果你仍希望味道多一點，可以加點海鮮醬（即廣東甜醬）、醬油、五香粉、八角來醃鴨肚內部，便能增加香氣。
- 要鴨子燒起來顏色漂亮，可在上皮料中加點橙紅粉色素拌勻，但用與不用便見仁見智了。

- Although roasted ducks are commonly available, a homemade one is still worth trying.
- The main difference between a homemade duck and readily-made one is that body of the former one is not injected with air. Besides, it tastes lighter and is healthier as it is simply marinated with salt. For a stronger flavour, you may add some hoisin sauce, soy sauce, five-spice powder and star aniseed to marinate the interior of the duck.
- You may add some orange colouring to the glazing sauce to brighten it up.

香芒咖喱乾炒蝦球
Curry Prawns with Mangoes

- 由於芒果能中和辣度，所以使咖喱不會過辣。
- 芒果早切會變黑，而炒得太久又會變啡色不好看。為使芒果與蝦的熱度相同而又不會變色。在蝦泡油後，可以把芒果也泡一泡。
- 在最後兜炒時，可以下少許薄芡兜勻，入口便沒有那麼油膩。

- Mangoes can neutralize the spiciness of curry.
- If mangoes are peeled and exposed to open air for a long while, they will oxidize and become dark in colour. On the other hand, if they are stir-fried for too long, they will also turn brownish. To make both mangoes and prawns attain the same temperature without any colour changes, you may blanch mangoes in hot oil after blanching prawns.
- At the final stage of stir-frying, you may stir in a light thickening sauce to make the dish less oily.

陳皮紹酒焗乳鴿
Stewed Baby Pigeons with Shaoxing Wine and Dried Tangerine Peel

- 此菜特點是肉質口感夠滑、不乾、有酒的香醇和陳皮味,而且不會熱氣。
- 鴿最好選用妙齡的乳鴿,以不超過7兩重為佳,做好的鴿,口感會更滑。
- 乳鴿走油的時間不要太久,微黃即可。
- 乳鴿先以陳皮等料頭爆香才下調味,為使其入味。
- 大火燜5分鐘後返轉再燜5分鐘便會熟透,顏色也會均勻好看。
- 葱棄去,陳皮及薑保留切絲,吃時將其與汁料扒於鴿面上桌,賣相特別又美觀。

- The meat of pigeon is succulent with a touch of wine and dried tangerine flavour.
- Choose baby pigeons for their tender meat.
- Blanch pigeons in hot oil until lightly brownish.
- Stir-fry dried tangerine peel, ginger and spring onion with pigeons before adding in seasoning for a better taste.
- Stew it on high heat for 5 minutes, turn the pigeons over and stew for another 5 minutes until cooked and evenly coloured.
- Discard the spring onion. Cut the stewed tangerine peel and ginger into shreds, and mix them with the sauce before pouring over the pigeons for serving.

芝士焗蟹缽
Baked Crab Meat Bowl with Cheese

- 此菜其實是芝士釀蟹蓋的變身,只是用盅取代蟹蓋。
- 蟹蓋焗太久易脆易爛,顏色不美,所以要食用時才焗。但用盅便可早點放入盅內焗,只要焗盤底放一點水,焗的時間久了一點也不會乾。
- 麵撈是用了多量牛油炒製的,放上麵包的作用,能吸去部份油份,麵包也香脆可口。但怕肥的朋友便不要吃麵包了,以免影響健康。

- Crab shells are easily broken, unattractive and have to be baked right before serving. Therefore, this dish uses bowls as containers instead. By placing some water in the baking tray, bowls of crab meat can be put into the oven earlier on and will not become dry after baking for a long while.
- Stir-fried batter is made by stir-frying large amount of butter. Bread is added in order to absorb part of its oil content and make it more crunchy and delicious.

魚羊燒鮮
Fried Mutton in Fish

- 魚和羊合起來便寫成「鮮」字，很早便聽說魚羊的配搭是鮮味一絕，一直也沒有品嚐過。後來決定自己做來個大測試，果然不同凡響。
- 俗語謂"汁不酸，魚不鮮"，所以做這個菜色要用酸甜汁為妙。
- 醃料用的十三香，可能較難買到，如在內地便很多地方都有售。但如果沒有，可以用八角粉、茴香粉、五香粉等與醃羊的香料拌勻便可。
- 最後要以平底鑊煎炸魚，較容易煎得香脆，如用炒鑊便比較困難。

- Fish and lamb make up the word "freshness" in Chinese and it is said that the two types of food complement each other in cooking. This dish is an exemplar of such a saying.
- The sweet and sour sauce is used to bring out the flavour of fish.
- The 13 spices of the marinade is widely available in mainland China. If you cannot find them, you can simply mix star aniseed powder, fennel powder, five-spice powder and the spices for mutton marinade together.
- Shallow-fry the fish in a pan makes it more crispy.

香蕉火腩蒜子燜大鱔
Stewed Eel with Roasted Pork and Bananas

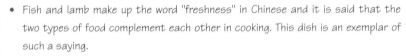

- 此菜非常好吃，但相信香港有很多人仍沒有品嚐過，吃過的人相信已有一大把年紀了。
- 鱔是越燜得久便越好吃。但香蕉不用太早加入。燜至水份餘¼杯才下香蕉燜3分鐘後，再焗一焗，鱔已經可以盡吸香蕉味道了。
- 燜好的香蕉顏色當然不好看，因此再以2隻香蕉切塊放入，開火把汁略滾起才上煲，那蕉味便會充足，並且顏色又美觀。

- It is a very delicious but old-fashioned dish which has never been tasted by the younger generation of Hong Kong.
- Eels take a long while to cook but not bananas. Add bananas to the stew when the sauce is reduced to ¼ cup, and then cover with a lid to cook for 3 minutes.
- The stewed bananas are dark in colour and mashy. You may zest up the dish by adding two more bananas in slices before serving.

麻辣雞丁
Spicy Stir-fried Chicken

- 我在西安時，在一所飯莊用膳，此為前菜小食，當時是用蒜心製作，十分可口。但此書拍攝期間沒有蒜心，我改用四季豆，如果蒜心當造時希望大家用回蒜心，會更好吃。但蒜心不用飛水，用四季豆才要飛水。
- 雞炸得乾身一些才好吃。麻辣的程度，視乎自己吃得多辣而定，喜辣者多放辣椒，要麻辣味多些的，又可以加多點花椒（但我建議大家加花椒粉，因為如吃時不小心咬着花椒粒，舌頭及口腔便受罪了）。

- In Xian, people make this dish with garlic shoots as an appertizer. However, during the shooting session of this book, garlic shoots are not available and I had to use beans instead. If garlic shoots are used, don't blanch them in hot water.
- Chicken has to be deep-fried until moisture is reduced. For spicy-food lovers, you may add more peppercorn to taste. (Peppercorn powder is recommended because peppercorn can make your tongue and mouth numb when bitten.)

黃金炒木須肉
Stir-fried Pork with Eggs

- 以蛋炒至金黃是為"黃金"，十分惹味。炒至乾身可以用來夾荷葉餅。如將其炒滑蛋，便是別一種風味。
- 用半肥瘦豬肉會比較香，如用瘦肉，口感粗糙亦欠甘香。
- 切絲時，宜粗幼適中，太粗太幼都不好。木耳亦是主角之一，切得太粗便不好吃。
- 如不想用太多油份，可以用易潔鑊來炒，如用鐵鍋，油便要多一點。
- 肉必定要泡油，炒時才會美觀，如用少許油兜熟，肉便不夠滑。

- Eggs have to be stir-fried until golden brown for a greater flavour.
- Use medium fatty pork for better texture.
- To save oil in cooking, use a non-sticky wok for frying.
- Meat has to be blanched in hot oil before stir-frying or it will become less succulent.

霸王豬肚
Braised Pig Abdomen with Glutinous Rice

- 與霸王鴨的做法差不多，只是改了用豬肚，此菜亦是懷舊菜式，現今的年輕人較少吃到。
- 豬肚必須要清洗得十分乾淨，否則會有異味。
- 其特色是以鹹蛋蓉及蟹黃作芡淋面，既美觀又可口。

- The making of braised pig abdomen is similar to that of braised duck. It is a traditional dish but is less popular nowadays.
- Pig abdomen has to be thoroughly cleaned or it will have a stinky smell.
- This dish features a topping sauce of salted egg yolk and crab roe which is delicious and attractive.

啤酒柱侯燜牛尾
Stewed Ox Tail with Beer

- 有點像德國式的西餐，但卻有濃厚的中菜風味，因用上醬油及中式醬料。
- 如要啤酒味濃郁，注入的過面清水可完全改用啤酒。
- 1.5小時如不夠腍，可以多燜1/2小時。一般而言燜1.5小時再焗一會是已經足夠。
- 洋蔥不用太早加入，待牛尾燜好後，才爆香洋蔥一起兜勻。
- 除牛尾外，可以改用牛腩亦可。

- It is a traditional Chinese dish with a German taste.
- To make its beer flavour stronger, you may replace water with beer for stewing.
- If the ox tail has not been tenderized after stewing for 1.5 hours, you may simmer it for half an hour longer.
- Onion should be stir-fried and added to the ox tail after it is stewed.
- You may replace ox tail with beef brisket if you like.

薔薇梅姿
Double-boiled Rosy Shape Pork with Preserved Cabbage

- 此為功夫菜，以其造型像一朵朵薔薇花而得名。做此菜色手工要熟練，否則可能要浪費很多肉才做到12朵花。
- 花朵的大小隨意，一般用1.5斤至2斤肉必定可完成。
- 注意用中慢火燜肉1/2小時，醬汁必定要收稠。為了容易切到此形狀，1/2小時剛熟的肉最為理想。
- 切時肉必須已完全凍，最好放雪櫃中雪一下才切，否則切時會有困難，做不到好的形態。
- 食用時淋回煮沸的原汁，可以打薄芡，使其有光澤。
- 此菜可佐飯及饅頭，雖是腩肉卻不膩口。

- It is a beautiful but tedious dish, which requires skillful hands to make or lots of meat will be wasted in the flower making process.
- You can determine the flower size as you desire. Normally, 1 to 1.2 kg of meat will do.
- The meat must be simmered on medium or low heat for half an hour until the sauce reduced and the meat is easy to cut.
- To make the meat cool enough for cutting, you may chill it in a refrigerator for a while first. Otherwise, it will be difficult to cut and difficult to shape.
- Boil the original sauce and pour it over the dish before serving. You may also make a glazing topping with a light thickening sauce to give the dish a lustre.
- This dish can be served with rice or steamed buns.

竹葉青蔥香燒肉
Stewed Pork with Wine

- 此菜如燜東坡肉，但東坡肉不用炸。
- 上老抽色後，炸前要吸乾水份，不然炸時油份彈出易生危險。
- 上桌時，如找到新鮮竹葉同上便更為特色。

- This dish is similar to Dongpo Pork, except that its pork has to be deep-fried.
- After colouring the pork with dark soy sauce, it must be patted dry before deep-frying or hot oil droplets will come out.
- You may decorate the dish with fresh bamboo leaves if you have some.

醬燒紐西蘭羊鞍扒
Roasted Lamp Chop with Special Sauce

- 此為西菜中吃。特別在於一般醃汁是不要的，此處卻燴黑椒汁淋下，便特別香及好吃。
- 羊燒至多熟，隨各人喜好，要熟一點的便把燒的時間延長一點。

- It is fusion dish of the east and west. In Chinese cooking, the marinade is usually discarded after use but this dish uses the marinade and have it cooked with black pepper as a topping sauce.
- You may adjust the cooking time of lamb chop according to your own taste.

南瓜汁鮮菌翡翠苗
Assorted Mushrooms and Pea Shoots in Pumpkin Sauce

- 口感清爽，材料配搭適合減肥瘦身人士。
- 南瓜蓉的汁要濃稠適中，過稀或過稠都不好，推芡要薄。
- 雜菌要先飛水，能去異味。

- This is a light dish, specially good for people on diet.
- The pumpkin purée sauce can neither be too thick nor too thin. Just a light thickening sauce will do.
- Blanch the mushrooms in hot water to remove their grassy smell.

岐山羊肉湯
Qi Shan Mutton Soup

- 我在西安一些街坊式的小館吃過，感覺不錯。此湯有補效，適宜天氣寒冷時飲用，用的是白參，補效較溫和，如用高麗參，相信熱底體質人士不宜。
- 此湯可放些泡饃（是不用發酵的麵糰，蒸熟待凍後撕成小粒，放入碗中，加入羊肉湯同吃，是當地人的特色）。

- This soup is very nutritive and is specially suitable to be taken in cold weather. It is recommended to use white ginseng for its moderate nature.
- You may also add in some non-fermented dough to this soup. (Steam the non-fermented dough to cooked, leave it to cool before tearing into tiny pieces, and then add in the soup. Add in mutton and serve).

乳花石湯丸
Marble Glutinous Rice Balls

- 曾在尖沙咀一所酒店的中菜廳中吃過，是餐單的單尾，當時並非叫乳花石湯丸，此名只是我覺得看似乳花石才取。
- 此湯丸可用多種不同的顏色，但必須要保留一份白色，因每一種顏色都混一點白色才可突出其色彩。色素是食用的色素，不是常吃，不會影響健康。
- 餡料我建議用芝麻餡，會較香。但拍攝期間，由於時間緊迫，來不及製作餡料，附近亦沒有賣黑羊酥的店舖，所以改用豆沙。其實用甚麼餡料隨自己喜愛便好。
- 湯丸必定要浸於水中，但不要用糖水，白開水便可，由於餡料是甜的，用糖水不能顯出湯丸的美味，淡的便好。

- This dessert is inspired by one made by a hotel in Tsim Sha Tsui.
- You may use different colours as you like but you must mix them with a portion of white colour to strike a contrast. Use edible colouring once in a while will not cause any harm to our health.
- It is recommended to use sesame paste as filling for its enticing aroma. Of course, you may use any other fillings as you desire.
- Soak the glutinous rice balls in clear water but not sweet soup, which will overtake the sweetness of the rice balls.

上湯素魚翅餃
Artificial Shark Fin Dumplings in Broth

- 材料中有紹菜或椰菜。單用馬蹄肉而不用菜也可以，只要把馬蹄肉加成4粒便可。
- 馬蹄肉拍扁後略剁，不要切粒，會影響口感。
- 煮餃子，水要大滾，放入餃子後不要攪動，當再滾起時加入1杯凍水，水再1次滾起時，浮起的餃便熟，可以撈起。
- 肉攪透後，放入雪櫃中略雪，除了包餃時較好包，口感也比較爽。

- If you just want to use water chestnuts without Chinese cabbage, you have to add 4 more water chestnuts to the ingredients.
- Smash water chestnuts before chopping it into fine pieces.
- Cook dumplings in boiling water but don't stir. When the water is boiling, add in 1 cup of cold water, wait until it boils again and then take out the floating dumplings.
- Chill the mince pork in a refrigerator to give it a firm texture.

魚翅菇瑤辦麵
Shark Fins and Mushrooms with Chinese Fettuccine

- 可用乾麵餅、生麵或伊麵製作。
- 麵條可預早煮開，但必須過冷後再隔乾水份備用。要注意：只用冷水沖一會便可，切莫把麵條浸在水中太久，否則會過臉。如煮開後立即使用，便無需過冷。
- 辦麵與炒麵的製作略有不同，口感各異。炒麵是把麵條灼開後，先炸脆放碟上，再把材料淋在上面。辦麵則不用再炸，直接煮材料芡淋面，口感比較清爽，沒有那麼油膩。

- Any kinds of Chinese noodles will do.
- Boil the noodles in hot water until loosened, and then rinse them with cold water for just a short while before straining off excess water. Don't rinse the noodles for too long or they will become too soft. If you use them for cooking right away, no rinsing is required.
- If fine egg noodles are used, you have to blanch them in hot water and then deep-fry in hot oil until crispy before serving with sauce. On the other hand, no deep-frying is needed for broad egg noodles.

黃金蟹苗炒飯
Fried Rice with Crab Roe

- 蟹苗者，"蟛蜞膏"是也。
- 禮雲子亦是蟛蜞子，但口感不一樣，蟛蜞膏比較軟身。
- 蟛蜞膏比大閘蟹膏更可口，珠海坦州一帶產量最多，每年農曆6月13日前後的1個月最為肥美，此段時間，蟛蜞會從河流游回大海中，錯過此時段，便要待來年才可吃到。捕魚人士會設網阻其入海，捕捉後生拆，以缽頭蒸熟出售。
- 以蟛蜞膏炒飯，甘香無比，加入薑米能去腥味，且食味匹配。
- 除炒飯外，亦可煮汁打芡，如製作石榴包便是。

- The addition of fine ginger dices can remove the fishy smell of crab meat and make the dish more delicious.
- Other than making fried rice, crab roe can also be added to thickening sauces for some other dishes.

平湖嫣翠
Steamed Egg with Crab Meat

- 利用涼瓜汁來蒸滑蛋，入口甘而清爽，喉嚨舒服。
- 蒸的時不用太久，8分鐘即可，以牙籤插於蛋中，牙籤不倒蛋已熟。
- 金箔與蟹黃放面即可。蟹肉亦可放涼瓜汁蛋液中同蒸，如何做任隨尊便。

- Steam eggs with bitter melon juice has a soothing effect on throat.
- Steam eggs for 8 minutes and then test the egg custard with a toothpick to see if solidified.
- Place gold foil and brown crab meat on the surface. You may also steam crab meat with eggs and bitter melon juice if you like.

野葛菜水
Yellowcress Tea

- 香港灣仔的"三不賣"，以專賣獨沽一味野葛菜水而聞名。價格由當年的五仙，加至現在的七至八元一碗，貴了不少。但物有所值，嚐得到很用心製作，材料選擇一絲不苟，很好喝。
- 野葛菜水的功效除了可以清熱、除煩、對筋骨痠痛、煙酒過多都有療效。一個月煲1次飲用，有保健作用。
- 野葛菜有乾品和新鮮的，買到新鮮的當然更好，但要注意根部必須清洗乾淨，用乾品則要浸透才好。亦可加入龍脷葉同煲。
- 有些人愛加鹽調味，我獨愛原味。

- A historical shop for Yellowcress Tea in Wanchai makes the best of its kind in town. The price has risen a lot from its original price at 5 cents per bowl decades ago to 8 dollars nowadays. Anyway, it is still prepared in meticulous care and is worth every penny of it.
- It is a soothing drink which can relieve physical pain and ease one's mind, and is good for heavy smokers and drinkers as well. It can be taken once a month as a healthy beverage.
- Yellowcress is available dried or fresh. For the fresh vine, you must clean its roots thoroughly. On the other hand, if you have bought a dried one, you must soak it in water until softened. You may also boil it with dragon's tongue leaves.
- Some people like to add some salt to taste.

上湯竹笙釀蘆筍
Bamboo Fungus and Asparagus in Broth

- 這是個清淡的菜色，迷你的BB鮮蘆筍，很容易買到。
- 如感覺麻煩，或沒有時間。蘆筍可以與竹笙同煮便可，無須穿入竹笙內。

- You can use fresh young asparagus available to make this refreshing dish.
- If you don't have time, you don't need to put Bamboo Fungus rings on asparagus. Simply boil asparagus with Bamboo Fungus together.

肉桂紅棗茶
Cinnamon and Red Dates Tea

- 選用外國出產的肉桂枝較香，但價錢較貴。
- 肉桂與紅棗、薑片同煮2分鐘後熄火。剛熄火時水較混濁，待一會沉澱後，水會轉清。
- 此茶韓國人特別喜愛，凍飲可口。如燒烤後感覺熱氣，喝此茶能清熱去肥膩。

- Imported cinnamon is more expensive but more fragrant.
- Boil cinnamon, red dates and ginger together for 2 minutes and then turn off the heat. Just leave it for a while, the murky tea will become clear.
- It is a favourite beverage of Koreans and can be served cold. This drink can relieve the febrile sickness caused by eating deep-fried or roasted food.

杞子桂花糕
Matrimony Vine and Sweet osmanthus Pudding

- 此糕為馬蹄糕之變身。但食味比馬蹄糕更清香，加入紅色的杞子，更搶眼奪目。
- 此糕之漿水要稀糊狀才做得好，糖水滾後要熄火才拌入漿，若太滾入漿便成稠糊狀，欠缺美感。
- 此糕應凍食，但不可放雪櫃，因雪過的桂花糕，顏色暗啞，不會晶瑩剔透，因此以室溫放涼便可。吃時亦無需煎。

- Its making is similar to water chestnut pudding but it is even more fragrant and brighter with the addition of Matrimony Vine.
- The liquid for this pudding has to be in a light porridge form which is added to the boiling sweet soup with the heat turned off. It cannot be poured in when the soup is too hot or it will become too thick and hard.
- This pudding must be served cold but cannot be chilled in a refrigerator as chilling will damage its translucency. Just leave it to cool at room temperature.

紅棗南瓜盅
Steamed Red Dates in a Pumpkin

- 此為健康天然，甜味來自南瓜之甜品。因此南瓜必須選夠甜才好。
- 南瓜與紅棗皆去核，除了因吃時方便之外，還有不去核會較燥熱之故。

- It is a healthy dessert with the natural sweetness of pumpkin. Therefore, we must select a sweet pumpkin for this dish.
- Both pumpkin seeds and red dates cores must be removed to prevent febrile sickness.

蜜汁心太軟
Glutinous Rice Balls in Honeyed Red Dates

- 此甜品的特點在於將糯米粉糰釀入紅棗中，先蒸後炸，才放入蜜糖中快手兜勻。是個簡單易做並可口的甜品，我在西安飯莊吃過後很喜愛，所以介紹給大家。

- Stuffing glutinous rice balls in red dates is the special feature of this snack. The stuffed dates are then steamed, deep-fried and finally coated with honey. It is easy and tasty.

附錄
APPENDIX

各種肉類醃料份量及時間
Amount of Seasonings and Time Needed for Marinating Meat

調味料 Seasoning 1/2斤 (catty) 300克(g)	醬油 soy sauce	糖 sugar	鹽 salt	生粉 cornflour	蛋白 egg white	酒 wine	薑汁 ginger juice	水 water	熟油 cooked oil	胡椒粉 pepper	時間 time
	茶匙 tsp*	茶匙 tsp	茶匙 tsp	茶匙 tsp	茶匙 tsp	茶匙 tsp	茶匙 tsp	茶匙 tsp		茶匙 tsp	分鐘 minute
豬 pork	1	½		1		½	½	1	1茶匙 1tsp		30
牛 beef	1	1		1		1		1	1湯匙 1tbsp**	少許 small	60
羊 mutton	1	½		1		1	1	½	1湯匙 1tbsp	¼	60
雞 chicken		½	¼	1	1	1	½	½	2茶匙 2tsp		30
鴨 duck	1	½		1		½	½	1	1湯匙 1tbsp	少許 small	30
鴿 dove	1	½		1	1	½	½	1	2茶匙 2tsp		30
魚 fish		½	½	½	2	½	½		1湯匙 1tbsp		15
蝦膠 shrimp colloid			¼	2	1				½湯匙 ½tbsp		15
蝦肉 shrimp			¼	½	1						15

*tsp = teaspoon

**tbsp = tablespoon

常用換算表
Conversion Tables of Common Units

1 常用材料換算表 CONVERSION TABLE OF COMMON INGREDIENTS

材料		
牛油 butter	1湯匙 = 14克 1量杯 = 227克 = ½磅 = 2小條	1 tbsp = 14g 1 cup = 227g = ½ pounds = 2 small strips
植物牛油 margarine	1湯匙 = 14克 1量杯 = 227克 = ½磅	1 tbsp = 14g 1 cup = 227g = ½ pound
生油 light soy sauce	1湯匙 = 14克 1量杯 = 227克 = ½磅	1 tbsp = 14g 1 cup = 227g = ½ pound
牛奶 milk	1湯匙 = 14克 1量杯 = 227克 = ½磅 = 奶粉4湯匙+水 = 奶水½量杯+水	1 tbsp = 14g 1 cup = 227g = ½ pound = 4 tbsp milk powder and water = ½ cup milk and water
蛋（連殼）egg (with shell)	1個 = 60克	1 = 60g
蛋（不連殼）egg (without shell)	1個 = 50克	1 = 50g
蛋黃 yolk	1個 = 20克	1 = 20g
蛋白 egg white	1個 = 30克	1 = 30g
細砂糖 sugar	1量杯 = 200克	1 cup = 200g
糖粉 icing sugar	1量杯 = 130克	1 cup = 130g
麵粉 flour	1量杯 = 120克	1 cup = 120g
生粉 鷹粟粉 cornflour	1湯匙 = 12.6克	1 tbsp = 12.6g
奶粉 朱古力粉 milk powder/chocolate powder	1湯匙 = 7克	1 tbsp = 7g
碎朱古力 ground chocolate	1湯匙 = 7克	1 tbsp = 7g
花生醬 peanut butter	1湯匙 = 7克	1 tbsp = 7g
蜂蜜 honey	1湯匙 = 21克 1量杯 = 340克	1 tbsp = 21g 1 cup = 340g
碎乾果 ground nuts	1量杯 = 114克	1 cup = 114g
葡萄乾 raisin	1量杯 = 170克	1 cup = 170g
乾酵母（依士）yeast	1茶匙 = 3克	1 tsp = 3g
鹽 salt	1茶匙 = 5克	1 tsp = 5g
發粉 baking powder	1茶匙 = 4克	1 tsp = 4g
蘇打粉 baking soda	1茶匙 = 4.7克	1 tsp = 4.7g